JOHN BROWN

Other titles in the **Americans—The Spirit of a Nation** *series:*

EDGAR ALLAN POE
"Deep Into That Darkness Peering"
ISBN-13: 978-0-7660-3020-6

FREDERICK DOUGLASS
"Truth Is of No Color"
ISBN-13: 978-0-7660-3025-1

HARRIET TUBMAN
*"On My Underground Railroad I Never
Ran My Train Off the Track"*
ISBN-13: 978-0-7660-3481-5

JESSE JAMES
"I Will Never Surrender"
ISBN-13: 978-0-7660-3353-5

JIM THORPE
"There's No Such Thing as 'Can't'"
ISBN-13: 978-0-7660-3021-3

JOHNNY APPLESEED
*"Select Good Seeds and Plant
Them in Good Ground"*
ISBN-13: 978-0-7660-3352-8

AMERICANS
THE *Spirit* OF A *Nation*

JOHN BROWN

"We Came to Free the Slaves"

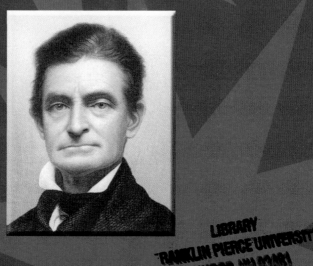

Anne Schraff

Enslow Publishers, Inc.
40 Industrial Road
Box 398
Berkeley Heights, NJ 07922
USA

http://www.enslow.com

"We came to free the slaves and only that."

Library of Congress Cataloging-in-Publication Data

Schraff, Anne E.
    John Brown : "We came to free the slaves" / Anne Schraff.
      p. cm. — (Americans-the spirit of a nation)
    Includes bibliographical references and index.
      Summary: "Examines the life of John Brown, including his childhood on the
frontier, his fight against slavery and the Harpers Ferry raid, his execution, and
legacy in American history"—Provided by publisher.
    ISBN 978-0-7660-3355-9
      1. Brown, John, 1800–1859—Juvenile literature. 2. Abolitionists—United
States—Biography—Juvenile literature. 3. Antislavery movements—United
States—History—19th century—Juvenile literature. 4. Harpers Ferry (W. Va.)—
History—John Brown's Raid, 1859—Juvenile literature. I. Title.
    E451.S34 2009
    973.7'116092—dc22
    [B]
                      2008054036

Printed in the United States of America

092009 Lake Book Manufacturing, Inc., Melrose Park, IL

10 9 8 7 6 5 4 3 2 1

To Our Readers:
We have done our best to make sure all Internet Addresses in this book were active and
appropriate when we went to press. However, the author and the publisher have no
control over and assume no liability for the material available on those Internet sites
or on other Web sites they may link to. Any comments or suggestions can be sent by
e-mail to comments@enslow.com or to the address on the back cover.

♻ Enslow Publishers, Inc., is committed to printing our books on recycled paper. The
paper in every book contains 10% to 30% post-consumer waste (PCW). The cover
board on the outside of each book contains 100% PCW. Our goal is to do our part to
help young people and the environment too!

Illustration Credits: Culver Pictures, Inc., pp. 83, 101; Enslow Publishers, Inc., p. 46;
Historic Photo Collection, Harpers Ferry NHP, pp. 60, 64, 88; Kansas Historical
Society, pp. 6, 10, 38, 49, 70, 82, 86, 91, 95, 103, 111; Library of Congress, pp. 9, 12,
13, 16, 17, 22, 25, 27, 33, 36, 50, 52, 55, 66, 71, 79, 92, 105, 112; Library of
Congress, North Carolina Division of Archives and History, Raleigh, p. 30; National
Archives and Records Administration, p. 42; North Wind Picture Archives, p. 35;
Virginia Historical Society, p. 62; West Virginia State Archives, Boyd B. Stutler
Collection, pp. 3, 45, 69, 70, 76, 97.

Cover Illustration: West Virginia State Archives, Boyd B. Stutler Collection (Portrait
of John Brown).

CONTENTS

John Brown

Escape to Canada

In mid-December 1858, fifty-eight-year-old John Brown took a bold step. He hated slavery so much that he decided to take slaves from their masters by force and lead them to freedom. Brown learned from friends that Jim Daniels, a Missouri slave, had a wife expecting a baby and two small children. The Daniels family was about to be sold to a Texas slave owner. Jim Daniels feared he might never see his family again. John Brown decided to take action.

On the night of December 20–21, Brown rode with twenty men into Vernon County, Missouri. At the Little Osage River, the party divided into two groups. Twelve went with Brown and eight with his friend Aaron Stevens. Both parties planned to liberate slaves.

John Brown went to the farm of Harvey G. Hicklan, who owned Daniels and his family. After tying up Hicklan and a houseguest, Brown forced Daniels, his wife, and children into an old wagon. He also took blankets and linens for the slaves.

At this time the Fugitive Slave Act was in force. It gave federal authorities more power to hunt down fugitive slaves who had escaped to free states and return them to their owners. This meant a fugitive slave was not safe within the borders of the United States. The only safety from slavery lay in escape to Canada.

Brown and his men next went to John B. Larue's farm. They took five more slaves and some food and clothing. Meanwhile, Aaron Stevens liberated a woman and killed her master in a gunfight. When the two parties reunited, between them they had freed eleven slaves from four families owned by different slave owners. They included Jim Daniels and his family, a widow with two daughters and a son, a young man and his brother, and a woman who had been forced to live apart from her husband.

A heavy snowstorm covered the tracks of the raiders as they headed for Kansas. There was now a price of three thousand dollars on John Brown's head. President James Buchanan had added another $250. The liberation of the eleven slaves made big news in the North. It was widely praised. Antislavery politician Gerrit Smith wrote, "Did you hear the news from Kansas? Our dear John Brown is invading Missouri."[1]

As Brown brought the slaves across Kansas, Jim Daniels' wife gave birth to a son. Daniels named the

After John Brown liberated eleven slaves from Missouri, President James Buchanan put a bounty on Brown's head.

boy John Brown Daniels. Brown led his little group of fugitive slaves from safe house to safe house. These were houses of antislavery people who sheltered and gave aid to fleeing slaves. Like Brown, they hated slavery and were part of the abolition movement. Abolitionists wanted to end all slavery in the United States.

In January, Brown's group found shelter at the Sheridan home near Topeka, Kansas. The slaves were poorly clothed and some had no shoes. They shivered in the cold. John Brown too suffered from the cold but he said, "Do not bother me. There are others not so well supplied."[2] The Sheridans found warmer clothing and shoes for the party, and treated them to a hearty meal.

This portrait of Sam Harper and his wife, two of the slaves liberated by John Brown in 1858, was taken in Windsor, Canada, in 1894.

Before leaving the Sheridan house, John Brown told Mrs. Sheridan, "We must be gone to-night. There is a great work before me—greater than I can tell, and you may never see me again, but you will hear."[3]

In Iowa, other abolitionists welcomed John Brown and the slaves with food and shelter. During much of the journey, armed men on horseback, eager to recover the slaves, had pursued them. But Brown's party managed to escape. They left Chicago in a boxcar and arrived in Detroit. There they boarded a ferry that would take them across the Detroit River to Canada and safety. Brown had brought the slaves more than eleven hundred miles, in eighty-two days, over rugged roads, through rain and snow. Now he bid them an emotional goodbye. He said he could now die in peace: "The arm of Jehovah protected us."[4]

> "There is a great work before me—greater than I can tell, and you may never see me again, but you will hear."

But John Brown would not die in peace. He was about to embark on his most daring effort to end slavery in the United States. The passion to end slavery, which drove him to such drastic actions, had been instilled in him as a child.

2

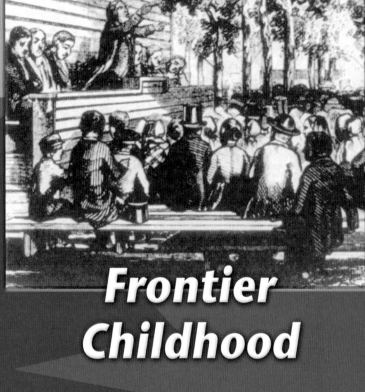

Frontier Childhood

John Brown was born on May 9, 1800, in Torrington, Connecticut. His mother, Ruth Mills, came from a deeply pious Calvinist family. The Calvinists, a Protestant sect that called the Bible the source of all truth, believed that obeying God's law was more important than obeying man's law. Ruth Mills's earliest ancestor in the United States was Peter Wouter Van Der Meulen, who came from Amsterdam. Wouter's son, Peter, changed the family name to Mills. Peter's son, Gideon Mills, was a lieutenant under George Washington during the Revolutionary War.

Father of a Rebel

John Brown's father, Owen Brown, was one of eleven children. As a boy, Owen was small for his age. He was frail and he stuttered. Owen's mother hired a slave named Sam who was from Guinea in Africa. Sam became the boy's best friend and protector, carrying him around on his shoulders. When Sam died, young Owen was heartbroken. Owen Brown's later hatred of slavery stemmed from his memories of Sam.

John Brown was born on May 9, 1800, in this house in Torrington, Connecticut.

Slavery

The institution of slavery was a fact of life in colonial America and in the early years of the United States. Black people continued to be bought and sold. Although Britain banned all slavery in its territories in 1833, in the United States from 1815 to 1860, the number of slaves increased. The introduction of the cotton gin increased the need for slaves. At the end of the War of 1812, some 250,000 bales of cotton were harvested in the South. In 1850, this had increased to 4.5 million. In 1859, the cotton kingdom stretched from the shores of the Atlantic Ocean in the east, to the Rio Grande River in the west, to the Ohio River in the north, and south in the Gulf of Mexico. It was one of the largest slave empires the world had ever seen in both the number of acres and the number of slaves. To many, this was a barbaric reality that needed to be changed.

When Owen Brown was five, his mother died. He was sent to live with his sister. Owen's sister, Asubah, raised him in a very strict Calvinist home.

Owen Brown learned the skill of shoemaking by age sixteen. He became a traveling cobbler, going from town to town and repairing shoes. At age twenty he met Ruth Mills. Two years later they married and lived in Norfolk, Connecticut. The first two children born to Ruth and Owen Brown died as infants. In 1798, a healthy daughter, Anna, was born.

At the time a religious revival was going on in Norfolk. Religious revivals were common at that time. A preacher would come to town, set up a large tent and, as the people gathered, he would urge them to repent and lead holier lives. Owen Brown eagerly attended the revival to learn more about what God wanted from him.

The revival preacher in Norfolk told the crowd to avoid sin and to follow God's law. Then he said that slavery was one of the greatest of all sins. Owen Brown already felt a kinship with black people from his friendship with Sam. But he did not think much about slavery until he heard the preacher describe what a great evil it was. Owen Brown immediately decided he would work to end slavery in the United States. He believed this was God's will for him. He began to work with the Underground Railroad.

Moving to the Frontier

As a small boy, John Brown was used to seeing his parents help fugitive slaves. When John Brown was five

A preacher speaking at a religious revival meeting in Eastham, Massachusetts. Owen Brown, John's father, attended a religious revival where he heard about the evils of slavery.

years old, the family moved to Hudson, Ohio, in an ox-drawn wagon. The Browns had four children, including eleven-year-old Levi Blakeslee. The Browns adopted the boy because he had lost his family.

The journey was long: forty-eight days. John Brown later described a "wilderness filled with wild beasts & Indians." He told of seeing "Rattle Snakes which were very large & which some of the company generally managed to kill."[1] For part of the journey, young John drove the wagon.

Owen Brown, John's father wrote, "When we came to Ohio the Indians were more numerous than the white

The Underground Railroad

The Underground Railroad was a series of stations or safe houses stretching from the southern United States north to the Canadian border. White people who opposed slavery and free black people offered their homes to fleeing slaves who traveled at night and hid by day when the slave catchers were active. The runaway slaves followed the North Star at night. The escapees were often referred to as passengers on the Underground Railroad. People like Owen Brown and other abolitionists were called conductors on the Underground Railroad.

The Underground Railroad helped many slaves escape to freedom.

people, but were very friendly, and I believe were a benefit rather than an injury." He added, "They brought us venison, turkeys, and the like."[2] Owen Brown had no sense of prejudice against any people.

> **Owen Brown had no sense of prejudice against any people.**

Owen Brown built a log house for his family. It had one large room as well as an upstairs loft where the children slept. The family lived on a diet of cornmeal mush, johnnycakes (cornmeal, milk or water), and bread.

Owen Brown opened a small tannery where the hides of animals were treated to convert them into leather. He soon built a larger house. The Browns raised their children to treat all people with respect. Many of the local white people did not like the American Indians, but the Browns treated the Indians respectfully.

A Childhood in the Wilderness

John Brown often played with the local American Indian children. He was even initiated into a tribe as a young buckskin. The Indians taught John how to dress animal skins into leather. He could make leather from the skin of squirrels, raccoon, wolves, and deer.

John spent many hours roaming through the woods, finding bird, squirrel, and turkey nests. He found one little bobtail squirrel and he took it home and made a pet of it. He tamed the squirrel and it followed him like a dog. But one day it vanished and John grieved for a long time. He searched for another bobtail squirrel but never found one. John was tender-hearted toward animals. He cared for a lamb for two years and again, when it died, he was grief stricken.

From earliest childhood John had been taught by his parents to "fear God and keep His Commandments," but often the boy was wild.[3] John later recalled that he was "*excessively* fond of the *hardest and roughest* kind of plays & could *never get enough* [of] them."[4] He liked to wrestle and get into snowball fights. The boys in Hudson formed into rival gangs and they challenged each other to snowball or fist fights. One time when John and his friends were getting the worst of a snowball fight, John ran hard at the rival boys and scared away a large group of them.

On December 9, 1808, John Brown's mother gave birth to a daughter. The infant lived just a few hours and Ruth Brown died soon after, leaving Owen Brown to raise six children. Later Owen Brown recalled the "remembrance of this scene makes my heart bleed now."[5] Within the year, Owen Brown married twenty-year-old Sallie Root. John Brown called her "a sensible, inteligent, and on many accounts a very estimable woman," but he continued to grieve for his mother and "never adopted her [Sallie Brown] in feeling."[6]

When John was twelve years old, the War of 1812 broke out between the United States and England. John's father provided horses and beef to the American army. John went along on many trips to army camps. The cursing of the American soldiers offended John and he decided he would never want to be a soldier.

A Passion Sparks

At this time an incident happened which dramatically changed John Brown's life. While his father supplied the army, John spent some time with the family of a United States marshal. The marshal's family had a twelve-year-old black servant who became friends with John. The boy showed John "numerous little acts of kindness" and they became close.[7] But John noticed that the marshal and his family liked him (John) and praised him for everything he did. But they treated the black boy harshly. John called the boy "fully if not more than his equal," but he was badly clothed, poorly fed, and frequently beaten with an iron shovel.[8] John Brown later cited this incident as making him a "most *determined Abolitionist* and led him to declare, or *Swear: Eternal war* with slavery."[9]

> John Brown later cited this incident as making him a "most *determined Abolitionist* and led him to declare, or *Swear: Eternal war* with slavery."

The plight of black slave children deeply moved John Brown. "The wretched, hopeless condition of *Fatherless* & *Motherless* slave *children*" broke his heart, "for such children have neither Fathers nor Mothers to protect & provide for them."[10]

At age sixteen, John Brown publicly accepted Jesus Christ as his Lord and Savior. His father had worried that this might never happen, because the boy was a rebel. But from that day on, John Brown read the Bible every day.

When John was seventeen, he and his younger brother went back to New England. They enrolled in a Massachusetts school run by a relative. While John enjoyed reading, he was never a scholar. He studied rhetoric (the art of convincing speech), grammar, mathematics, Latin, and Greek. Later, he went to Morris Academy in Connecticut. But John became ill in the middle of his studies and had to return home. He never resumed his formal education, but he read constantly.

At eighteen, John Brown was five feet, ten inches tall, with thick dark hair brushed straight back. He had blue-gray eyes, and his face was gaunt with hollow cheeks. He had a serious personality and a bad temper. He was a skilled tanner and surveyor (measuring and noting property lines), and he farmed. John was honest and did excellent work, but he was very stubborn in his dealings with people. He thought he was right and he defended his position with blunt words. Many people did not like him because of his harsh speech. For this reason he was not as successful as he might have been with a more pleasing personality.

Slaves Back to Africa

In 1817, the American Colonization Society was formed in the United States. With government and private funding, the society hoped to establish a colony in Liberia in Africa where American slaves could be sent. There the slaves would be free. Some members of the society wanted to send all blacks to Liberia, but others just wanted to send some of the slaves in the hopes of weakening slavery in the United States.

Returning American slaves to Liberia would have been difficult for many reasons. American-born slaves had never lived in Africa, where the society was organized tribally. African people lived in large communities like the American Indians lived in before the Europeans arrived. It would have been hard for the freed slaves to adjust to this way of life.

Owen Brown, John Brown's father, was an ardent abolitionist and his views had a tremendous impact on John.

Owen and John Brown were against this idea. They believed it was unfair to deport the slaves to Africa. Slaves had worked hard in America and contributed to the growth of the American economy. The Browns believed the slaves should be freed and allowed to live in the United States like everybody else.

When he was twenty, John Brown became a conductor on the Underground Railroad along with his father. He worked at his father's tannery, but he was eager to be on his own. So he and his brother Levi Blakeslee went into business together. They moved to the outskirts of Cleveland, Ohio, and opened a small tannery.

At this time John Brown spent all of his free time reading. He memorized the Bible, and read *Aesop's Fables,* the life of Benjamin Franklin, *Pilgrim's Progress,* and the hymns of Dr. Isaac Watts. He preferred books from which he could learn something new. He also sought the company of older men, respecting their wisdom. Young men his age seemed silly and shallow to John Brown.

Abolitionists

John Brown was not alone in his passion. The Quakers objected to slavery and demanded its abolition in the late seventeenth century. They denounced the buying and selling of human beings. Other Americans joined the abolition crusade after the American Revolution. Many prominent Americans joined in the relentless campaign to put an end to slavery, including William Lloyd Garrison and Henry David Thoreau. However, fervent abolitionists were pelted with rotten eggs and stones in many American cities in the north. Garrison himself was led around Boston with a rope around his neck by proslavery activists. Yet the number of abolitionists grew—from the hundreds to the hundred thousands.

John Brown regularly read materials condemning slavery. Tracts attacking slavery were produced by the Quakers starting in the 1700s. John Woolman, a New Jersey Quaker, wrote protesting against slavery, as did physician Benjamin Rush in 1773. Fueled by his reading, Brown's hatred of slavery grew stronger.

John Brown broke the law to help slaves escape. He firmly believed slavery was a sin against God and therefore he had every right to break man's laws that allowed it. He believed slavery was such a terrible sin that it simply could not be allowed to persist.

John Brown's passion to end slavery became the central mission of his life.

Chapter 3

Marriages and Business Ventures

Business was good at the tannery run by John Brown and Levi Blakeslee. Brown did the cooking until more employees were added. For the job of cook and housekeeper, Brown hired the widow Mrs. Amos Lusk. She was well known in the area for making and selling good bread, which Brown often bought.

Marriage

Mrs. Lusk brought her nineteen-year-old daughter, Dianthe, to help. She was devoutly religious and caught John Brown's attention immediately. When Dianthe Lusk went into the woods she often sang hymns and prayed. Brown was attracted to her piety and he asked her to marry him. After a brief courtship, the young couple was married on June 21, 1820.

Brown later described his wife as "*remarkably plain,* but neat, industrious & economical girl; of excellent character; earnest piety, & good, practical common sense." A year younger than Brown, she had "a most powerful & good influence over him."[1] Brown noted that when his wife gave him advice she did it in a kindly way and never aroused his temper.

Dianthe Lusk Brown had a family history of mental problems. She was mostly stable and dependable, but at times she became confused. Brown did not complain about her spells of nervousness. On July 25, 1821, their first child, John Jr., arrived. The tannery did well and Brown added even more employees.

Strict Businessman and Family Man

Though a young man, John Brown controlled his family and his employees with a firm hand. When he caught an employee stealing, Brown did not call in the law. He dealt with the situation himself. He forbid anyone to speak to the thief for two months, keeping him in silence as punishment for his crime. Brown had a strong,

John Brown moved his family to Richmond, Pennsylvania. He built this tannery in 1826.

domineering personality and his family and employees obeyed him.

On January 19, 1823, a second son, Jason, was born. On November 4, 1824, Owen was born. John Brown moved his wife and three sons from Hudson, Ohio, to Richmond, Pennsylvania, a small village in Crawford County. Brown wanted more land for his growing family. He cleared twenty-five acres of woodland and built a new tannery. In October 1825, he was again in business and supporting his family.

Brown's tannery was two stories high with eighteen vats. Dianthe Brown kept house for her family and cooked for the growing number of tannery employees. Her health was fragile. Her nervous spells became more frequent.

A Loving Father

On January 9, 1827, a fourth son, Frederick, was born. He was a sickly child, suffering from constant headaches. Having an ailing child was even more of a burden to Dianthe Brown. John Brown was a good father who was stern with the children when they misbehaved, but tender with them when they were ill. He often sat up all night comforting a sick child in his arms, rocking back and forth. One of his sons later recalled a typical evening in the Brown house. Brown would sit before the fire and take the children, one, two, or three at a time onto his lap. He would talk to them or sing with them until bedtime. He had a favorite hymn, "Blow Ye The Trumpet Blow," and he sang it with the children over and over.

> He had a favorite hymn, "Blow Ye The Trumpet Blow," and he sang it with the children over and over.

John Brown showed great compassion to young and sick animals as well. When a lamb was born and showed weakness, he carried it into the house, bathed it, and wrapped it in a blanket, spoon-feeding the animal until it revived. He saved many newborn lambs this way, even those near death. Brown's children noticed their father's sympathy for weak and abused animals and people and they copied him.

On February 18, 1829, the Brown's first daughter was born. Years later, Ruth Brown recalled her earliest memory of her father. After she had been baptized, her father wiped her wet face with a silk handkerchief with yellow markings on it. "I thought how good he was to wipe my face with that pretty handkerchief. He showed a great deal of tenderness in that and other ways."[2]

The Browns' son Frederick died as a small child. On December 21, 1830, another son was born and Brown named him Frederick as well. (The family followed a common custom of naming a subsequent child after one who had died.)

John Brown was very interested in promoting the town where he lived. He supervised the construction of a common school to serve his children and those of his neighbors. He also became town postmaster.

Hatred of Slavery Grows

The Browns lived in a large two-story log house, one of the largest houses in town. Brown formed a partnership with a relative, Seth B. Thompson, who lived in Hartford, Ohio, thirty miles away. Thompson sold the hides Brown tanned. John Brown was doing well financially, and was respected as a dynamic young leader. But in the midst of his business success, his passion against slavery was inflamed by a violent event in Virginia— Nat Turner's Rebellion.

John Brown had the same religious beliefs and passionate hatred of slavery as Nat Turner. Both men read the Bible daily. Both knew it by heart. Both saw themselves as chosen by God to end slavery.

John Brown built a special room in his house to be used as a hiding place for runaway slaves. He taught his

Nat Turner's Rebellion

A massive slave uprising led by black abolitionist Nat Turner took place in 1831 in Southampton County, Virginia. Turner claimed to hear voices urging him to begin a widespread slave insurrection. In a single day, sixty white people were killed. A terrified South reacted with extreme force. A battle between Turner's followers and government troops claimed the lives of more than one hundred slaves. Born a slave in Virginia on October 2, 1800, Turner was intelligent. He performed scientific experiments and read long passages from the Bible. He believed he had been chosen to lead a black army of slaves to overcome slavery in the United States. Six weeks after the rebellion began, Turner was captured. He was executed along with sixteen followers.

Nat Turner (standing center) led a slave uprising in Virginia in 1831. Many people were killed during the battle and Turner was eventually executed. The violent event inflamed Brown's hatred of slavery.

children to show kindness to black people. His daughter, Ruth, was so moved by his example that she wanted to ask black strangers to move in with her family.

Brown began thinking more and more of what he could do to help African Americans. He thought about building a school for free black children in Ohio.

Family Tragedy

In 1832, Dianthe Brown was pregnant with her seventh child. She suffered from heart trouble and "childbed fever," complications of pregnancy. Dianthe Brown gave birth to a son on August 7, but he soon died. Dianthe Brown called her husband and children to her bed. She spoke of going to heaven and seeing her son Frederick, who had died recently, and other relatives who had died. On August 10, 1832, she died.

John Brown sunk into a deep depression after his wife's death.

John Brown sunk into a deep depression after his wife's death. She had been his faithful companion and he depended upon her. But with five children to support and a business to run, Brown was soon caught up in his duties. He had fifteen journeymen and apprentices working for him. They all had to be served daily meals. Brown hired the daughter of neighbor John Day to cook and clean for his family and his workers. Soon the work became too much for the young woman and she brought along her younger sister, sixteen-year-old Mary Day, to help.

Mary Day was a strong, silent, and hardworking girl. She had long, beautiful dark hair. She impressed John

Brown. Though he was thirty-three years old and she was only sixteen, he decided to ask her to marry him. Such a great difference in ages between husbands and wives was common at that time.

Brown wrote Mary Day a letter telling her that he wished to marry her. He handed her the letter. She did not know what was inside the envelope. She could not imagine what this stern man was writing to her. Later, one of her daughters recalled what her mother said she had done with that letter years before. Mary Day took the envelope "to her bed that night and slept with it under her pillow. The next morning she found the courage to read it."[3]

Mary Day read the marriage proposal but said nothing. When she went to the springs to get water for her chores, Brown followed her into the woods and asked for her answer. Mary Day told him she would marry him.

A New Wife

There were major differences between John Brown and Mary Day beyond the age gap. Brown was well read. He read *Napoleon and His Marshals*, Rollin's *Ancient History*, Jewish historian Josephus, and Greek historian Plutarch. Mary Day did not read many books. She was quiet and humble. He was strong-minded and confident. The couple was married on June 14, 1833. Ten months later, on April 11, 1834, their first child, Sarah, arrived.

In spite of her quiet personality, Mary Brown turned out to have great inner strength. She provided stability for John Brown. No matter what happened, she remained calm and dependable. She never complained and she was completely loyal to her husband. She took charge of his children and soon they called her mother. John Brown held religious services in the family home every morning and Mary joined him. Each family member read a passage from the Bible. Brown stood to pray, always leaning slightly forward, his hand resting on the chair in front of him.

Mary Brown provided great stability for Brown and his family. The couple married in 1833.

On October 7, 1835, John Brown welcomed his second child, Watson, with Mary Brown. The Browns moved back to Hudson, Ohio, with the big family squeezed into a small rented house. John Brown and his son John Jr. built a new tannery in 1836. On October 2, 1836, son Salmon was born. Along with his work at the tannery, Brown became more involved with the Underground Railroad. He regularly took runaway slaves along a segment of the railroad. He hired a free black couple to work at his house and tannery. This led to a major rift between John Brown and the rest of the white community in Hudson.

On Sunday, the Browns always sat in a pew near the front of their church. John Brown expected his two black employees to sit with him and his family, but they were asked to sit in the back of the church. When Brown defiantly led the couple to his pew, many in the church were outraged. The Brown family was soon expelled from the congregation. Although John Brown remained fervently religious, he never again belonged to an organized church.

To earn more money, John Brown became a real estate speculator in Hudson. He bought parcels of land and planned neighborhoods. He arranged for streets to be put in and named them. He made a profit when the small lots were sold. Brown became an officer in the Cuyahoga Falls Real Estate Association. He also became a bank director.

On November 3, 1837, Mary and John Brown had their fourth child, Charles. In the same year, another violent racial tragedy fired up Brown's passion to do something dramatic to end slavery.

Murder of an Abolitionist

A white Presbyterian minister in Missouri, thirty-five-year-old Elijah Lovejoy, had been recently converted to the abolitionist cause. His church paper, the *St. Louis Observer,* called slavery a cruel sin. Angry white men invaded Lovejoy's office and wrecked it, smashing his press. Lovejoy and his wife were driven from St. Louis. They settled in Alton, Illinois, a small town overlooking the Mississippi River. Missouri was a slave state and Illinois was a free state, so Lovejoy thought he could safely carry on his antislavery crusade there.

Three times, from July 1836 to August 1837, mobs had broken into Lovejoy's office, scattered his supplies, and thrown his printing press into the river. Lovejoy was told to stop criticizing slavery or he would face disaster.

Elijah Lovejoy already had ordered his fourth press. It was delivered to a sturdy stone warehouse. Lovejoy remained there to guard his printing press. On November 7, 1837, another mob arrived. Unable to break into the warehouse, they climbed on the roof, setting it on fire. When Lovejoy appeared at the door he was shot five times. He died within minutes. The next morning a large mob jeered at his wife, Celia, and their young son, as Lovejoy's body was taken away for burial.

An angry mob attacked Elijah Lovejoy's office on November 7, 1837. Lovejoy's murder infuriated John Brown as the mob of attackers went unpunished.

John Brown was infuriated by Lovejoy's murder. What especially enraged him was that the murderers went unpunished. Until then, John Brown had fought slavery by helping runaway slaves on the Underground Railroad. Now he concluded this was not enough. He began to see all black people as part of his family, and his family was suffering. He saw himself as a patriarch, who would lead his people to freedom, just as Moses led the Jewish people from Egypt to freedom.

As John Brown became more focused on abolition, his economic fortunes declined. The 1837 economic depression in the United States caused many businesses

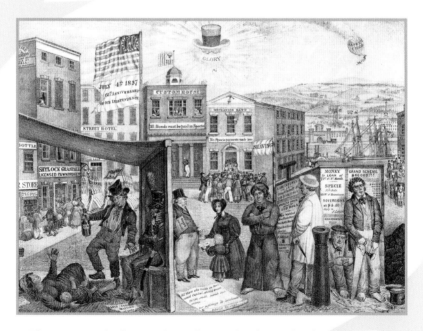

The economic depression of 1837 in the United States had a harsh effect on the Brown family. This political cartoon shows the difficulties many Americans faced during that time.

to fail. Banks went out of business and depositors lost their money. Brown could not sell the land he had developed. He was deep in debt. Creditors sued him for the money he owed them. At the edge of bankruptcy, even the tannery was failing for lack of business.

The Brown family struggled to survive. John Brown had five children from his first marriage and four young children from his second marriage. The eldest child in the group was sixteen-year-old John Jr. John Brown turned to yet another business venture in a desperate attempt to recover. He bought some sheep, hoping to make money selling wool. But while his head was filled with business plans, his heart was aimed at ending slavery.

Chapter 4

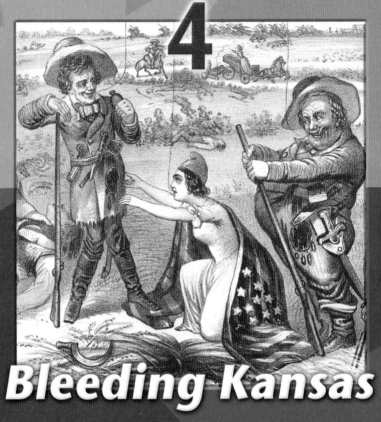

Bleeding Kansas

John Brown was desperate. A creditor got a court order to take his farm. Brown believed the order was illegal and he resolved to fight it. Brown and his three sons, nineteen-year-old John Jr., seventeen-year-old Jason, and sixteen-year-old Owen decided to hold off the sheriff and his men when they came to take the farm. The plan failed. John Brown and two of his sons were arrested and taken to the Akron jail. John Brown's hatred of the government only increased. The same government that took his farm also permitted the cruel system of slavery. The Browns spent the night in jail.

In the middle of this economic ruin, the Brown family continued to grow. On March 9, 1839, son Oliver was born. On December 7, 1840, Peter was born. In 1841, the Brown family possessions were sold at auction. The Brown family farm in Hudson was gone, along with most of their furniture and livestock. The Browns were allowed to keep eleven Bibles, two horses, two hogs, ten hens, two cows, some small pieces of furniture as well as clothing and tools. John Brown now pinned all his hopes on his new sheep business in Richfield, Ohio. Brown's business partner was Herman Oviatt, who had a large herd of sheep. Brown tended the sheep and he did an excellent job of it, reading up on the care of sheep and becoming an expert.

In 1842, the Browns were at last free of debt as a result of success in the sheep business. They made a new start in Richfield. On September 14, 1842, Mary Brown gave birth to her seventh child, Austin. John Brown opened another tannery to earn extra money and he was starting to win prizes at the county fairs with the sheep he had raised. He built a reputation as a hardworking man who knew the sheep business. However, in the midst of this hard-won success came an incredible family tragedy.

Another Family Tragedy

On September 4, 1843, Charles Brown, a sturdy little five-year-old, was stricken with dysentery, a serious disease causing vomiting, diarrhea, dehydration, and sometimes death. It is sometimes linked to impure food or water. Charles died and during the next week, nine-year-old Sarah, three-year-old Peter, and baby Austin also died from the disease. Salmon Brown was seven at the time and he later recalled the tragedy as "a calamity from which Father never fully recovered." John Brown himself remembered having "a steady, strong desire to die," and join his children in heaven.[1]

> Salmon Brown was seven at the time and he later recalled the tragedy as "a calamity from which Father never fully recovered."

On December 23, 1843, daughter Anne was born. On June 22, 1845, Amelia was born, and on September 11, 1846, Sarah II was born. Once more tragedy struck. On November 8, 1846, baby Amelia died in a scalding accident.

John Brown's unshakable religious faith helped him endure these terrible losses and go on with his life. He believed that a heavenly reunion with loved ones awaited him. On the deaths of his children Brown wrote, "This has been to us all a bitter cup indeed, and we have drunk deeply, but still the Lord reigneth and blessed be his great and holy name forever."[2]

A New Business Plan

Meanwhile, John Brown developed a plan, which he hoped might make his sheep business successful. He believed that large mills underpaid the sheep raisers and unfairly controlled the price of wool. Brown wanted all the sheep raisers to band together and establish a central office in Springfield, Massachusetts. Brown would be the broker making deals and setting fair prices for different grades of wool. The wool from some sheep is of higher quality than others and should bring a better price. Brown's sheep were of good quality. At the time, Brown wrote articles for wool industry publications and he had become well known as an expert.

Brown wanted to grade wool in nine different categories with the best wool getting top dollar. Again Brown ran into trouble. The British wool industry flooded the market and brought down world prices.

In March 1846, the Browns moved to Springfield, Massachusetts. Brown was now the official representative for Ohio's wool sellers. At forty-six, Brown was wiry and straight shouldered.

At that time, word spread throughout the black community that there was a prominent white wool broker who cared deeply for the plight of slaves. Many blacks were amazed that such a white man existed. Frederick Douglass, a former slave who became a famous writer and orator, was one of the most important black leaders in the United States. He heard about Brown and he was eager to meet him.

Meeting Frederick Douglass

When they finally met in 1847, Douglass expected to find Brown living in a fine home. He was surprised

Frederick Douglass (above) met John Brown for the first time in 1847 in Springfield, Massachusetts.

to find him in a plain house almost bare of furniture. Brown invited Douglass to sit at the crude, unvarnished dinner table and share the usual family fare of beef soup, cabbage, and potatoes. Douglass found Brown "singularly impressive," with "bluish gray eyes full of light and fire."[3] Douglass further noted that Brown "fulfilled St. Paul's idea of head of the family. His wife believed in him, and his children observed him with reverence."[4]

In their conversation, Brown bitterly denounced slavery and told Douglass he wanted to create an armed force in the heart of the South to free the slaves. He said the men would be in small groups and they would hide in the Allegheny Mountains between raids on the plantations. (The Alleghenies, part of the Appalachian Mountain range, stretch from northern Pennsylvania south through Maryland, West Virginia, and Virginia.) Brown believed that many slaves would rise up and join the armed force when they heard of the raids. Douglass was stunned by Brown's passion. "Though a white gentleman," Brown was, in Douglass' words, "in sympathy a black man and as deeply interested in our cause, as though his own soul had been pierced with the iron of slavery."[5]

Douglass was trying to end slavery by peaceful means, but Brown insisted only bloodshed could end the institution of slavery.

In April 1849, another of the Brown children fell ill. Ellen was a year old when she got a cold, which turned into pneumonia. John Brown carried her around day and night. She died in his arms. He calmly closed her eyes, folded her arms, and put her back in her cradle. But, at Ellen's burial, Brown "sobbed like a child."[6]

John Brown's wool business was going under. In a last-ditch effort to save it he took a trip to England, hoping to sell his bales of wool at a good price. There, British buyers ripped open the bales and ridiculed the quality of Brown's wool. Brown returned to the United States a failure.

Moving to North Elba

In 1849, the Browns moved to North Elba near Lake Placid in a remote part of New York's Adirondack Mountains. The Browns' farm had five cows, four oxen, some pigs, sheep, and chickens. North Elba was a multicultural community with many African-American families. These free black people had been living in cities and were seeking a simpler life. Brown socialized with them as equals. He addressed black men as "Mister," and black women as "Missus." Such courtesy from white people was unusual.

Kansas-Nebraska Act

On May 25, 1854, the Kansas-Nebraska Act passed the United States Senate after months of bitter fighting between antislavery and proslavery forces. The act laid out procedures for governing these new territories in the midwestern United States. The territories would be able to vote if they wanted to be slave states or free states. Nebraska was always expected to be free because it was farther north. But Kansas, next to slave state Missouri, seemed likely to be a new slave state.

In 1852, Mary Brown had another son, who lived just twenty-one days. Then, on September 25, 1854, the last child born to Mary and John Brown arrived—Ellen II. In that same year, in Kansas momentous events occurred, which would dramatically change the life of John Brown.

In October 1854, four of John Brown's adult sons decided to move to Kansas. Word had gone out that land was cheap and fertile there. The Reverend Samuel Adair, husband of John Brown's sister Florilla, had already settled in Kansas. His farm was on Osawatomie Creek, a lush spot where the Pottawatomie Creek flows into the Osage River. John Brown Jr. and his wife, Wealthy, along with Jason and his wife, Ellen, went there first. Frederick and Salmon soon followed. The families pooled their resources. The Brown sons sent letters to their parents praising Kansas. By May 1855, the Browns who had gone to Kansas were all living at Osawatomie, two miles from their uncle's place. They named the settlement Brownsville.

Kansas Battles Over Slavery

According to the terms of the Kansas-Nebraska Act, the people of Kansas were about to choose their territorial

John Brown Jr. and his wife, Wealthy, were the first from the Brown family to move to Kansas in 1854.

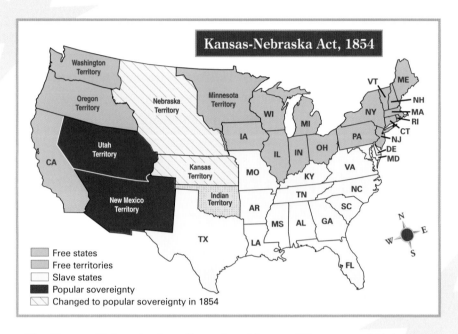

The Kansas-Nebraska Act allowed residents of Kansas and Nebraska to decide whether or not they wanted slavery within their territories. This map shows the slave states and free states in the U.S., and how this act affected the new territories.

legislature. This was the governing body that would decide if Kansas would be free or would permit slavery. There were about two thousand men living in Kansas who were legally permitted to vote. But proslavery Missourians, nicknamed border ruffians by the abolitionists, entered the state on election day to cast illegal ballots. Missouri senator David Atchison personally led a group of eighty Missourians across the border. He told his followers, "There are eleven hundred coming over from Platte County (Missouri) to vote. And if that ain't enough we can send five thousand—enough to kill every abolitionist in the territory." The proslavery vote numbered 5,427 and the free soil vote was 791—4,908 votes were illegally cast.[7]

Outraged abolitionists complained to Governor Andrew Reeder. He went to President Franklin Pierce who dismissed all charges of fraud. The election stood. "Now let the southern men come on with their slaves . . . we are playing for a mighty stake," boasted Senator Atchison. "If we win we carry slavery to the Pacific Ocean."[8]

The new proslavery legislature soon passed tough laws against abolitionists in Kansas. All speech against slavery became illegal. Anyone caught with abolitionist literature could be found guilty of a felony. Anyone helping a slave escape from his master could be executed. In order to enforce these rules, Missourians carried weapons and searched for abolitionists and drove them from the territory.

Brothers Henry and William Sherman, nicknamed Dutch Henry and Dutch William because they were from Germany, were typical of the proslavery element in Kansas. William Sherman warned, "The day is soon coming when all the damned Abolitionists will be driven out or hanged."[9]

In October 1855, free-state settlers in Kansas called their own convention in Topeka, seventeen miles west of Lawrence, Kansas. Now Kansas had two territorial legislatures, each claiming to be the legal government.

John Brown Jr. wrote letters to his father describing the violent situation in Kansas. Although free soilers, many from New England, were also moving into Kansas, they were outnumbered by the proslavery Missourians.

John Brown Jr. wanted to form free-state militias to defend the abolitionist families. He pleaded with his father to send arms.

John Brown was torn between his obligations to his younger children in North Elba and his desire to help his older sons with a cause he also supported. Eventually he left twenty-year-old son Watson with his wife and the younger children, and he headed for Kansas. Watson continued farming to keep the family fed.

John Brown Moves to Kansas

Now fifty-five years old, his hair graying, and his face well lined, a stooped John Brown still had a lot of energy. He needed little sleep and could outwork men half his age.

Brown found his sons and their families living in miserable conditions. A harsh winter was coming and no cabins had been built. The families were living in flimsy tents. As driving rain and wind lashed the tents, men, women, and children huddled together shivering.

> **John Brown still had a lot of energy. He needed little sleep and could outwork men half his age.**

John Brown immediately took charge. When he arrived, the fields and gardens were unfenced and cattle trampled the crops. Brown led his sons in a harvest of all the pumpkins and squash that were left. Then they gathered wild grapes and hickory nuts. They built cabins for Jason, John Jr., and their families. Freezing

LIBERTY, THE FAIR MAID OF KANSAS_IN THE HANDS OF THE "BORDER RUFFIANS".

Although many free soilers moved to Kansas, the proslavery Missourians greatly outnumbered them. This political cartoon depicts proslavery politicians harassing Liberty, a representation of the Kansas Territory.

weather set in before more cabins could be built. John Brown directed his sons to drive stakes in the ground on three sides of a half-built building. They stuffed prairie grass in as insulation. When the full force of winter came, temperatures dropped to twenty degrees below zero. Thanks to John Brown's firm leadership, they all survived.

In 1856, Owen Brown, John Brown's eighty-five-year-old father, died. It was an emotional and financial blow. He had sent as much money as he could to his children and grandchildren. Though John Brown did not see his father often, they remained close allies in the abolition movement.

The ruins of the Free State Hotel after the sack of Lawrence by proslavery forces. This event pushed John Brown to take action against slavery.

Further events of 1856 pushed John Brown into desperate action. In May, seven-hundred-and-fifty armed Missourians swarmed into Lawrence, Kansas, to loot and burn the town because it was a symbol of a free Kansas. John Brown led a thirty-four-man militia to try to save the town, but as he headed there he was met by a messenger with bad news. Everybody in Lawrence had fled before the Missourians arrived. It became known as the "sack of Lawrence." Brown was outraged that no defense of Lawrence had been made.

President Franklin Pierce again made it clear that he was on the side of the proslavery legislature in Kansas. He called the Topeka legislature illegal and authorized federal troops to help the proslavery forces remain in power.

The Final Straw

Then an incident in Washington, D.C. convinced Brown once and for all that the forces supporting slavery could commit any outrage they chose and not be punished. On May 22, 1856, Massachusetts Senator Charles Sumner delivered a passionate speech against slavery and the violence in Kansas. He titled his speech, "The Crime Against Kansas." He used strong language, denouncing the Missourians as "hirelings picked from the spew and vomit of an uneasy civilization."[10] In his speech Sumner attacked proslavery Senator Andrew Butler of South Carolina. Butler's nephew, Representative Preston Brooks of South Carolina, was so angry at the insult to his uncle that he beat Sumner with a cane on the Senate floor. Sumner survived the attack, but Brooks was never prosecuted.

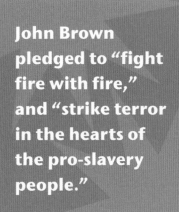

John Brown pledged to "fight fire with fire," and "strike terror in the hearts of the pro-slavery people."

John Brown had now come to believe that the only way to overcome the violence being committed on behalf of slavery was to use violence. He thought that the antislavery forces would not be taken seriously if they continued to lose every battle. He thought of the murdered Elijah Lovejoy, of free-state families in Kansas run out of the territory, of the attack on Lawrence, and now a bloody and beaten Senator Sumner. John Brown pledged to "fight fire with fire," and "strike terror in the hearts of the pro-slavery people."[11]

5

The Killings at Pottawatomie Creek

Sometime after arriving in Kansas and seeing the violence, John Brown resolved to make his stand against the proslavery men at Pottawatomie Creek. He chose his targets with care. Among them were the Sherman brothers, whose cabin was a kind of tavern and a meeting place for proslavery Missourians. He would also be looking for James P. Doyle and his sons, William and Drury. Doyle served on the local grand jury and William was a bailiff. The Doyles were from Tennessee and they hated abolitionists. Allen Wilkinson was a district attorney in the proslavery local court. He was also from Tennessee. These men were well known to Brown as enemies of a free Kansas. Brown saw them as part of the conspiracy that delivered Kansas into slavery and terrorized those who opposed them.

John Brown assembled his raiding party. Seven men would join him, including four of his sons and son-in-law Henry Thompson, husband of Ruth Brown. The Brown sons were Owen, Frederick, Salmon, and Oliver, the youngest. The two other men were James Townsley, a local painter, and Theodore Weiner. None of these seven men had ever committed a serious crime.

Brown's First Attack on Slavery

At sundown on May 23, 1856, a wagon carried seven of the men toward Pottawatomie Creek. John Brown walked alongside the wagon. As darkness settled in, the eight men made camp. They were one mile north of Henry Sherman's cabin. The next day, Saturday, May 24, they spent planning the raid. The attack would take place before the moon rose that night.

Heavily armed with revolvers and short cutlasses (straight broadswords, which Brown got from an Army officer in Ohio), the raiding party waded across Mosquito Creek to Pottawatomie. They arrived first at James Doyle's cabin. Recently Doyle had warned a free-state merchant to leave the territory or face death. As the raiders approached the cabin, they were charged by one of Doyle's bulldogs. James Townsley killed the dog and another bulldog fled into the woods. In the cabin were

James Doyle, his wife, Mahala, and their six children. When Doyle opened the door, five armed men rushed in, overpowering Doyle. The raiders said they were part of the Northern Army and they were taking him prisoner. Sons William and Drury were also captured, but when the raiders began to take sixteen-year-old John Doyle, his mother pleaded for her younger son's life. John Brown pushed the boy back inside the house and the raiders left with the three Doyles.

The three captives were led down the road about two hundred yards. There they were hacked to death with the swords. Although John Brown did not personally take part in the killings, he fired one shot into James Doyle's head.

The raiders then moved on to the cabin of Allen Wilkinson. He had issued many arrest warrants for free-state men. Mrs. Wilkinson related that on the night of the attack, just before they went to sleep, her husband had told her a raid against the antislavery forces was being planned. By the next weekend, "there would not be a Free State settler left on the creek."[1] When Allen Wilkinson went to the door to respond to a request for directions, the armed men entered. As they began taking Wilkinson away, his wife pleaded that he be allowed to stay with her because she was ill with the measles. John Brown told her the neighbors would help her, and they took Wilkinson away. The next morning Allen Wilkinson's body was found one hundred and fifty yards from the house.

In the final cabin attacked, James Harris was asleep along with his wife and child. Also in the cabin that

John Brown led a raiding party, including four of his sons, to Pottawatomie Creek where they murdered proslavery leaders.

night were William Sherman, John Wightman, and Jerome Glanville. When the raiders rushed in, Harris, Wightman, and Glanville were taken outside and questioned, one by one. They were asked if they aided the proslavery cause or if they had ever harmed free-state settlers. They all denied any such activities and they were not harmed. Then the raiders took William Sherman away with them. He was killed with swords at the edge of the creek.

The men then washed the blood from their swords in the creek and returned to their camp.

Aftermath of the Violence

Before the killings at Pottawatomie Creek, John Brown believed abolitionists were too peaceful and even cowardly. They had refused to defend Lawrence, Kansas, a fact that enraged Brown. They fled and left the town to the mercy of the attackers. Elijah Lovejoy's murder was not avenged. Sumner's brutal attacker was not charged. But now, because of this awful night, John Brown and his followers believed attitudes would change. Salmon Brown clearly noted this change: "That was the first act in the history of Kansas which proved to the demon of Slavery that there was as much

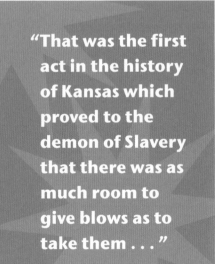

"That was the first act in the history of Kansas which proved to the demon of Slavery that there was as much room to give blows as to take them . . ."

room to give blows as to take them—It was done to save life, and to strike terror through their wicked ranks."[2]

In an effort to justify the Pottawatomie killings, John Brown, Jr., said, "that blow was struck for Kansas and the Slave; and he who attempts to limit its object to a mere settlement of accounts with a few pro-slavery desperadoes on that creek, shows himself incapable of rendering a just judgment in the case."[3]

In the South, John Brown became a feared omen of violence that might come. The killings in Kansas were denounced as the merciless slaughter of innocent, unarmed men. John Brown was denounced as a brutal murderer.

After the killings, John Brown and his sons went to Uncle Samuel Adair's cabin. He allowed John Jr. and Jason in, but he condemned the others as murderers and refused to let them in. Even John Brown's sons had regrets. Owen cried in remorse at what had been done. Jason Brown, who had not been in the raiding party, asked his father, "Father, did you have anything to do with that bloody affair on the Pottawatomie?" John Brown responded, "I approved of it," adding, "God is my judge. The people of Kansas will yet justify my course."[4]

Proslavery Forces Fight Back

The proslavery Kansas court indicted John Brown and his sons and fellow raiders on charges of murder. Posses hunted them and when John Jr. went into the countryside he was captured by Missourians. He was beaten and put in chains and marched to a prison camp. Already shaken by what had happened at Pottawatomie, the imprisonment undermined John Brown Jr.'s mental health. His brother Jason was also captured and held in a prison camp, though neither John Brown Jr. nor Jason Brown had participated in the raid. Jason was eventually released and John Brown Jr. was able to flee from captivity.

On August 30, 1856, a band of Missourians surrounded Samuel Adair's farm. Frederick Brown had been staying there and they were looking for him. When Frederick Brown came out of the house and walked toward the Missourians, he was shot in the head and fell dead.

Between 1856 and June 1857, John Brown became a hunted criminal. But he was also becoming a celebrity.

Harpers Ferry

President George Washington decided to establish a new national armory at Harpers Ferry, Virginia, in 1794. He saw it as a good location because of the water power provided by the Potomac and Shenandoah rivers. In 1817, the United States government began to manufacture rifles at Harpers Ferry. The armory and arsenal produced weapons there until the outbreak of the Civil War in 1861.

To those fighting slavery he became a colorful hero. John Brown traveled north and began talking to trusted abolitionist friends about his plan to create an army of runaway slaves and abolitionists. He had chosen a likely target for his big operation—Harpers Ferry in Virginia.

A New Plan

John Brown believed if he could attack and seize a famous landmark such as Harpers Ferry, he could use it as a launching pad for his slave uprising. Once the slaves on the surrounding plantations heard of the uprising, he thought they would join in to create an army of abolitionists and runaway slaves. The army would hide in the nearby mountains after the initial strike at Harpers Ferry and from there they would conduct more raids, and be joined by more slaves, until the entire system of slavery in the South began to collapse.

John Brown contacted wealthy antislavery men, primarily in New England, hoping to get financial help for his plans. He needed ammunition and weapons. Many men helped John Brown, but there were six in particular, known as "The Secret Six," who supported him. Some knew of his specific plan to attack Harpers Ferry, while others had

> John Brown became a hunted criminal. But he was also becoming a celebrity. To those fighting slavery he became a colorful hero.

This is a view of Harpers Ferry, Virginia, taken around 1865. Harpers Ferry became the next site for Brown's crusade against slavery.

just partial information. But all six shared Brown's passionate hatred of slavery and his determination to end it. They gave money and moral support to Brown up to the fateful day when he attacked Harpers Ferry.

Using funds he received from The Secret Six, John Brown got a new weapon—a two-edged bowie knife attached to a six-foot pole. A blacksmith made the weapon for him. Brown ordered one thousand of these pikes to be used in the upcoming slave uprising. He saw the pike as a perfect weapon for the slaves as they escaped from their masters. The slaves were untrained in the use of guns. The pikes were simple to wield and deadly.

In August 1857, Brown returned to Kansas to find the situation there settled politically. Although the

The Secret Six

Gerrit Smith had been a United States Representative from New York. He fought against slavery on the floor of Congress. In a letter to John Brown dated December 30, 1856, he wrote that he knew of John Brown's bravery and "your self-sacrificing benevolence, your devotion to the cause of freedom, and have long known them. May Heaven preserve your life and health, and prosper your noble purposes!"[5]

Thomas Wentworth Higginson was a minister. He was a world traveler with deep admiration for the people of Africa. It outraged him that they were slaves in America.

George Luther Stearns was a wealthy lead pipe manufacturer who lived with his wife, Mary, in a mansion in Medford, Massachusetts. Mary Stearns saw Brown as a hero and a prophet.[6]

Franklin Benjamin Sanborn grew up in a strongly abolitionist New Hampshire family and was an admirer of Ralph Waldo Emerson and other antislavery writers.

Samuel Gridley Howe was a doctor, widely admired for his work on behalf of the blind and deaf. He found ways to teach the blind to read, write, and play musical instruments. He hated slavery for its cruelty to helpless people.

The sixth man was the Reverend Theodore Parker who first met Brown in 1857 when Brown heard one of his powerful sermons against slavery. Parker was willing to support whatever John Brown planned to end slavery.

All six of these white men were educated and intelligent. They became close friends and allies of John Brown, offering him money and moral support to end slavery.

John Brown used a two-edged bowie knife attached to a six-foot pole to create a weapon called a pike. This would be used in the Harpers Ferry raid. The bowie knife (above) was taken from Brown during the attack on Harpers Ferry.

proslavery legislature still ruled, the free-state sentiment had grown and by 1861 Kansas would be admitted to the Union as a free state.

Harpers Ferry

His actions no longer needed in Kansas, John Brown focused all his attention on the attack on Harpers Ferry. He believed this would have a dramatic effect that would change the course of history. He felt that within the first twenty-four hours of the attack his army would swell with hundreds of runaway slaves. They would all flee into the Allegheny Mountains and from there conduct raids on other areas, always gathering more volunteers until they formed a large army.

Brown believed this would create an atmosphere of terror in the South. The Southern slave owners would see their cause was lost. Slavery would be weakened all over the South. At this point, Brown thought his abolitionist friends in the North would succeed in passing legislation abolishing slavery all over the United States.

Brown saw the violence he would unleash at Harpers Ferry as a minor blood-letting compared to the eventual cost in lives if a Civil War had to be fought over the issue of slavery.

In November 1857, John Brown began recruiting soldiers in Kansas for his raid on Harpers Ferry. At the same time, proslavery supporter Charles Hamilton, an emigrant to Kansas from Georgia, forced eleven free-state men into a ravine, killing five. This killing spree motivated John Brown to mount an attack on Missouri plantations where he successfully rescued eleven slaves and took them to freedom in Canada.

Chapter

The Road to Harpers Ferry

In the summer of 1859, John Brown visited New England to meet with members of The Secret Six and his abolitionist friends. He went to Concord, Massachusetts, to speak at the town hall. The audience was filled with judges, wealthy people, and famous writers like Henry David Thoreau and Ralph Waldo Emerson. John Brown received moral and financial help from these sympathizers in the battle against slavery, including from some black abolitionists such as Jermain Lougen and James Gloucester.

New England: Seedbed of Reform

New England was the American center of the spirit of reform in the 1800s. Many causes were supported, including women's rights, better treatment for the insane, prison reform, and abolition. It was the issue of abolition that stirred the most passion. By 1850, there were many abolitionist societies in New England. Though their members were often heckled, stoned, and even lynched, nothing stopped them. Ralph Waldo Emerson and Henry David Thoreau were the most prominent spokesmen for the cause. Thoreau's writings, such as *Walden*, were hailed all over the world. Emerson was a world-famous poet and philosopher. In New England, more than in any other place, John Brown was considered a hero.

Watching John Brown speak at Concord reminded Emerson of how much he admired this man. Emerson wrote in his diary about Brown: "He is a man to make friends wherever on earth courage and integrity are esteemed."[1] Comparing him to the heroes of the Revolutionary War, Thoreau said John Brown was "like the best of those who stood at Concord Bridge once, on Lexington Common, and on Bunker Hill."[2]

Heading for Virginia

Encouraged by his friends, John Brown left New England and headed for Connecticut to pick up the custom-made pikes he expected his army of runaway slaves to use. Brown was moving fast now. He returned to North Elba in June 1859 for a final visit with his family. He asked his sons to join him for the raid on Harpers Ferry. Salmon and Jason Brown refused. Jason was still troubled by the events at Pottawatomie Creek. Salmon, though fiercely abolitionist, did not believe the raid would work. Daughter Ruth's husband, Henry Thompson, also refused to join. John Brown Jr. was suffering from another bout of depression so he could not go. The only sons willing to join their father were thirty-five-year-old Owen, twenty-four-year-old Watson, and Brown's youngest son, twenty-year-old Oliver. But even these three had serious doubts about the success of the raid. Oliver Brown went to Harpers Ferry and looked it over and concluded it could not be captured with a small force of men. Eventually though, Oliver convinced the other two

Salmon Brown, one of John Brown's sons, refused to take part in the Harpers Ferry raid. He did not believe the attack would be successful.

brothers to come: "We must not let our father alone."[3] So three sons joined John Brown in the plan to raid Harpers Ferry.

Another Meeting With Douglass

John Brown also wanted Frederick Douglass to be a part of the project. He asked Douglass to meet him at an old stone quarry in Chambersburg, Pennsylvania, in August 1859. Brown was staying nearby, using the name Isaac Smith and pretending to be a cattle buyer. Frederick Douglass came to the meeting along with a runaway slave named Shields Green. They all sat on the stones in the quarry one night to discuss Harpers Ferry. After Brown explained all the details of the raid, Douglass said Brown was "going into a perfect steel trap, and that once in, he would never get out alive; he would be surrounded at once, and escape would be impossible."[4] Douglass argued that "only national force could dislodge slavery."[5]

John Brown pleaded with Douglass to change his mind. "Come with me Douglass," he said. "I will defend you with my life. I want you for a special purpose. When I strike, the bees will begin to swarm, and I shall want you to help hive them." Douglass refused.[6]

Frederick Douglass and Shields Green had come together to the quarry meeting from New York. As Douglass prepared to leave he asked Green if he was coming. Green said he was not—he was joining John Brown's attack on Harpers Ferry. So Douglass left alone.

John Brown was convinced that all the efforts of his abolitionist friends in New England to end slavery by peaceful means would come to nothing. Something dramatic needed to happen. Harpers Ferry was just fifty-seven miles from Washington, D.C. The attack would send shock waves through the political world and start the revolution that would end slavery.

On August 25, 1859, Secretary of War John B. Floyd received an unsigned letter warning that John Brown of Kansas planned to attack a federal armory in Maryland from Harpers Ferry. Since there was no federal armory in Maryland, Floyd discounted the letter and took no action.

Finalizing His Plans

John Brown began assembling his army at a small farm on the Maryland side of the Potomac River, about five miles from Harpers Ferry. Brown's daughter Annie and daughter-in-law Martha Evelyn (Oliver's wife) did the cooking and housekeeping for the group. Brown had gathered twenty-one men. Among them were five black men. The black volunteers included Dangerfield Newby. A tragic personal story drove him to join this raid. Born of a Scottish father and a slave mother, Newby was himself freed by his father. But his pregnant wife, Harriet, and their seven children remained in slavery. Newby had tried to earn enough money to buy their freedom, but he could not. Harriet Newby was about to be sold to a slave owner in New Orleans and Newby feared he would lose his entire family.

This is the small farmhouse John Brown rented to use as his headquarters for the Harpers Ferry raid. This image of the Kennedy Farmhouse was taken around 1860.

Another black volunteer was John Anthony Copeland, a twenty-two-year-old free-born North Carolinian. His Uncle, Lewis Sheridan, was also a free black volunteer. Perry Anderson, a free black from Pennsylvania, had met Brown in Canada. Finally there was Shields Green who had escaped slavery in South Carolina after his wife died. He had left his son behind in slavery and he was determined to join the fight for abolition.

Most of the men in John Brown's army were in their twenties. They were passionate in their support of John Brown's cause. As the day of the attack came near, the Brown women, Annie and Martha, were sent home to North Elba. John Brown then called his men, one by one, to take an oath of obedience to the cause and receive their commissions. The three Brown sons were made

Shields Green, a runaway slave, joined Brown after hearing about the plan in a meeting with Brown and Frederick Douglass.

captains. The other men were named lieutenants. The five black men, lacking military or firearm experience, were privates.

The pikes, Sharps rifles, and revolvers were loaded on wagons. John Brown shaved off his white beard and announced that the time had come to move.

On Sunday, October 16, 1859, a cold rain was falling. John Brown held a religious service for his army. He asked one of the black volunteers to lead it. The final loading took place, filling a heavy wagon and a smaller one. John Brown climbed onto the seat of the smaller wagon. "Men, get on your arms," Brown called out, and his men fell in line. As the wagons moved through the steady rain, there was total silence. "We will proceed to the Ferry," John Brown said.[7]

The attack on Harpers Ferry was underway.

Dangerfield Newby, a freed slave, volunteered for Brown's raid. He had been trying to buy his family's freedom, but could not afford it.

Chapter

7

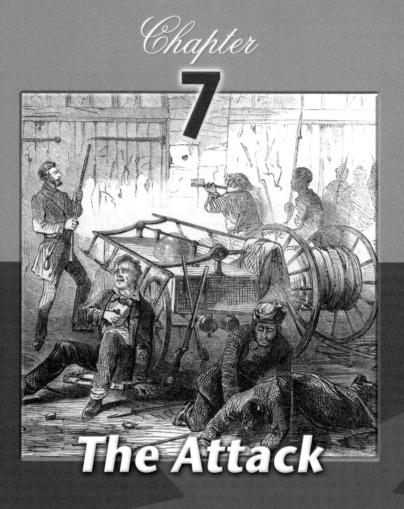

The Attack

John Brown and his men crossed the bridge over the Potomac River. As they approached the Virginia side, they encountered the watchman who patrolled the bridge. They took the man prisoner. Then they headed for the armory gate. They broke it open with a crowbar and rushed inside. John Brown sent his men to various locations within Harpers Ferry. Brown and his men took the virtually unguarded facility without opposition. He and his men moved around the buildings with ease.

Brown left some of his men within the rifle works. With his remaining men he took over the engine house. Before midnight, Harpers Ferry was completely under the control of John Brown.

Taking Hostage a Famous Descendant

John Brown was pleased with how smoothly everything went. He sent some of his men into the surrounding countryside to capture white slave owners and free their slaves so they might join in the uprising. A very attractive target was the plantation of Colonel Lewis Washington, a great-grandnephew of George Washington.

Four of Brown's armed men pushed their way into Washington's home. They told Washington they had come to free the slaves of the South. Brown's men forced Washington to give up some of his prized possessions—the pistol that the Marquis de Lafayette had given to George Washington during the American Revolution and a sword belonging to Frederick the Great of Prussia.

Washington was taken to Harpers Ferry and guarded by one of the black volunteers. When John Brown and Lewis Washington came face to face, Brown told him why he had been captured: "I wanted you particularly for the moral effect it would give our cause having one of your name as a prisoner."[1]

As word spread into the countryside that plantations were being raided, John Brown expected he would soon be joined at Harpers Ferry by jubilant slaves escaping their captivity. But the reaction of slaves freed by Brown's raiders was confusion and fear, not rejoicing. John Brown was a white man and the slaves considered whites to be their oppressors. Many thought Brown was a slave owner who had come to take them to a harsher place in the Deep South. In earlier slave rebellions, such as the one led by Nat Turner, the slaves accepted a black liberator. But most could not believe a white man like John Brown had come to rescue them from slavery. Many did not even understand what the raids were all about and, in their bewilderment, they simply fled and hid.

A Train Arrives at Harpers Ferry

At 1:00 A.M. the express train from Baltimore made its customary stop at Harpers Ferry. The train usually discharged and took on passengers at the Wager House, a train station and hotel at the end of the bridge. The conductor on the night of October 16 was shocked to see armed men on the bridge. Hayward Shepherd, an African-American baggage handler on the express train, confronted one of Brown's armed men. Shepherd was shot and killed. He became the first to die in John Brown's raid on Harpers Ferry.

The train remained at Harpers Ferry while frightened passengers milled around. Nobody knew what was going on. Near dawn, Thomas Boerly, a white resident of the town of Harpers Ferry, was killed by a shot from the arsenal. As the sun rose, some of John Brown's men were getting nervous. They thought they would take the arsenal, make their point, and then retreat into the safety of the Allegheny Mountains. There was a sense of things beginning to go very wrong. The men wondered why John Brown was not leading them into the mountains now. They had made a bold attack against the government that permitted slavery. Staying seemed dangerous. Brown told his men to stand firm and await orders.

The Fatal Mistake

Messengers from Harpers Ferry hurried to nearby towns to sound the alarm about the raid. But it was a slow process. John Brown then made a fateful decision. He allowed the stalled railroad train to continue on its journey. The passengers quickly boarded and the train headed into the Ohio Valley. When they reached the town of Monacacy, the conductor fled into the telegraph office. He told the president of the Baltimore-Ohio Railroad, John W. Garrett, that armed men had seized Harpers Ferry. This sealed John Brown's fate. Garrett got in touch with Governor Henry Wise of Virginia, the commander of the Maryland National Guard, and the President of the United States, James Buchanan. The alarm went out. There was an armed uprising at Harpers Ferry. Black slaves, led by a white abolitionist, were in rebellion. It was a grave emergency.

Bells rang in the town of Harpers Ferry rallying every able-bodied man to join this fight to drive John Brown from the armory. By 11:00 A.M. October 17, volunteer groups were forming in the streets. The Jefferson Guards, a militia, assembled their weapons.

Some militiamen confronted Dangerfield Newby, who stood guard at the bridge. Newby was struck by a six-inch spike fired from a gun. He fell with a gaping neck wound and died instantly.

John Copeland and his uncle were surrounded by approaching militiamen and taken prisoner. Many of Brown's men were soon captured, wounded, or killed. Even John Brown finally realized that he could not overcome the forces against him. He sent one of his son-in-law's brothers, William Thompson, to ask for a truce. Brown hoped he and his men would be allowed to leave if they gave up the fight. Thompson was immediately captured. Then Brown sent his son Watson and another man under a flag of truce. Both men were shot on sight. Though gravely wounded, Watson made it back into the engine house.

Last Stand in the Engine House

Brown and his remaining men, along with their prisoners, including Colonel Washington, were inside the engine house. Brown barricaded the doors and windows. He cut portholes in the brick walls so his rifles could poke through to fire.

Every window in the engine house had been shattered. Hundreds of shots came through the doors. More and more men arrived to surround the engine house where John Brown made his last stand. Oliver Brown, rifle in hand, peered through a crack in one of the barred doors. He was shot and fell to the floor in great pain. He died about twelve hours later.

Four of the ten men killed at Harpers Ferry, including two of John Brown's sons: John Kagi (top left), A. D. Stevens (top right), Oliver Brown (bottom left), and Watson Brown.

Colonel Lewis Washington was an eyewitness to the last hours of the siege. He later said John Brown was the "coolest, and firmest man I ever saw in defying danger and death. With one son dead by his side, and another shot through, he felt the pulse of his dying son with one hand and held his rifle with the other, and commanded his men with the utmost composure, encouraging them to be firm and to sell their lives as dearly as they could."[2]

The town was filled with militia, volunteers, and men of every kind. They sniped at Brown's engine house fortress. Brown and his men fired back. All the saloons in Harpers Ferry were open and there was heavy drinking. Everybody knew John Brown was going to lose this battle. There was no more fear of him. The atmosphere was strangely festive in the town. The mood of the milling crowds ranged between anger at what John Brown had done and wild excitement.

> John Brown was the "coolest, and firmest man I ever saw in defying danger and death."
>
> —Colonel Lewis Washington

President James Buchanan ordered federal troops to go to Harpers Ferry and end the siege. In the late afternoon of October 17, Brevet Colonel Robert E. Lee and Lieutenant J. E. B. Stuart were on their way.

Lee and Stuart arrived at Harpers Ferry at 11:00 P.M. Lee ordered all the bars closed and the mobs of people sent home. At the crack of dawn, J. E. B. Stuart went to the engine house. The door opened a little. Stuart was

Robert E. Lee

Fifty-two-year-old Robert E. Lee was a graduate of West Point. He had been superintendent of the military academy. He had a long and impressive career in the United States Army. Lee personally believed slavery was evil. He inherited slaves from his mother, but he freed them and never had any of his own. Lee loved the United States and did not approve of the South seceding from the Union. Still, he loved Virginia more than he treasured the United States. When the Civil War broke out, Lee turned down President Lincoln's offer to head the Union troops. He accepted the command of the Confederate Army instead.

staring into the face of "old *Osawatomie Brown* who had given us so much trouble in Kansas."[3] Brown had a rifle in his hand and it was ready to fire. Stuart gave him Lee's note demanding immediate surrender. Brown rejected it and instead demanded that he and his men be allowed to leave peacefully.

Storming the Engine House

Stuart stepped aside and waved his hat in the air as a signal to his men. But Brown had closed the door and Stuart's men had to batter the locked door with

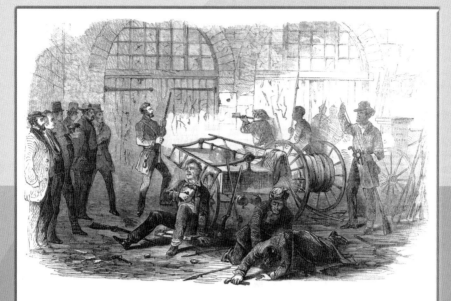

John Brown made his final stand at Harpers Ferry inside the *engine house (above). Outside, federal troops led by Colonel Robert E. Lee and Lieutenant J. E. B. Stuart prepared to storm the engine house, unless Brown would surrender.*

sledgehammers. It would not yield. Brown and his men fired at the attackers but did not hit anyone.

Lieutenant Israel Green was chosen to lead the attack on the engine house. He found a heavy ladder and ordered his men to use it as a battering ram. The door shattered, leaving a hole large enough for Green to enter, followed by his men. Green looked around for John Brown and when he saw him he leaped at him, sword in hand. Green was carrying his dress sword instead of his military saber, which was much more deadly. When the sword cut Brown, his body was thrust upward from the stabbing blow. The blade had struck Brown's belt buckle and it bent before making a deep wound. Now Green grasped his sword with both hands and slashed at Brown, striking him in the head. Bleeding heavily, John Brown crumpled to the floor. Watson Brown, gravely wounded, was still alive as John Brown was carried from the engine house. Watson suffered for another two days before dying of his wounds.

Of the twenty-two men who started out that rainy night for Harpers Ferry, ten had been killed. They included Brown's two sons, Oliver and Watson. Of the black volunteers, two had died. Five of the raiders were captured and jailed. Two escaped to be captured later. Five men escaped, including Owen Brown and a black volunteer, Osborne Anderson, who fled to Canada.

Taken Prisoner

The wounded John Brown was carried to the armory. News of the violent end of the raid on Harpers Ferry spread throughout the country by telegraph. Men who had supported John Brown or had been associated with him were fearful. The Secret Six, who had given moral and financial support to Brown, reacted in various ways. Amid fear and dismay, some burned all their letters from Brown and hoped their letters to him never turned up. In the immediate aftermath of what looked like a disastrous failure, there were few voices on behalf of John Brown.

At North Elba, there was shock and grief. The family had lost two sons, and their father was in jail awaiting a likely conviction and execution. Annie Brown, Brown's daughter, years later recalled the moment when the family learned what had happened. She described the family "struck dumb, horror stricken with grief too deep and hard to find expression in words or even tears."[4]

Though he had strongly opposed John Brown's raid on Harpers Ferry, and had refused to be a part of it, Frederick Douglass was known as a friend of John Brown. He never denied that. However, Douglass feared for his own life. He left the United States for Canada and eventually went to England.

Heartsick abolitionists wondered what would be the end result of the Harpers Ferry disaster. Would it link their cause with violence and sink their hopes for an end to slavery? Or in some strange way had Brown's defeat at Harpers Ferry been a victory in disguise?

Chapter 8

The Trial

John Brown lay on the armory floor on a pallet (a blanket placed on the floor as a bed). His feet were toward the fireplace. His head was propped up with pillows. His hair was so full of blood that it was impossible to see what color it was. When visitors began arriving, Colonel Lee asked Brown if he wanted to see them. Otherwise, Lee said, he would make sure Brown was not bothered. Brown said he was eager to speak to people because he wanted the truth to come out.

Speaking to John Brown

For three hours people streamed in—news reporters, politicians, some ordinary people. Virginia's Governor Henry Wise, a Democrat with ambitions to become president, was among the first to see Brown. He was curious about John Brown. After speaking with Brown, Wise observed, "They are mistaken who take Brown to be a madman. He is a bundle of the best nerves I ever saw; cut and thrust and bleeding, and in bonds. He is a man of clear head, of courage, fortitude, and simple ingenuousness."[1]

Many asked Brown why he attacked Harpers Ferry. "We came to free the slaves and only that," he said.[2] When asked if he was prepared to die for what he had done, he replied, "I am prepared to go."[3]

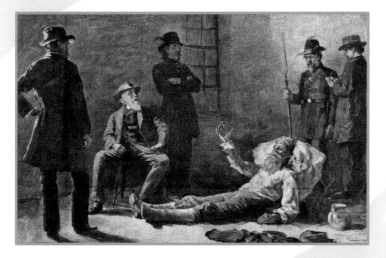

John Brown was taken to the armory after the raid ended. Many people came to talk to Brown and asked him why he had attacked Harpers Ferry.

Some of the questioners hoped to link Brown with the Emigrant Aid Society in New England. This antislavery group had sent free-state settlers to Kansas. Brown denied they helped him in any way. When asked about his sources of money and weapons, Brown refused to name anyone. He simply said he had acted alone.

> "If you seek my blood, you can have it at any moment without this mockery of a trial."

On Thursday, October 20, John Brown and four of his men taken captive at Harpers Ferry were sent to Charles Town, eight miles southwest of Harpers Ferry. Brown along with two white men, Aaron Stevens and Edwin Coppoc, and two black men, John A. Copeland and Shields Green, were delivered to the Charles Town jail.

The Trial Commences

On October 25, 1859, bayonet-carrying militiamen escorted John Brown and Aaron Stevens into the courtroom. Brown had difficulty walking and was assisted by militiamen on either side of him. Still, he held his head high and his eyes were filled with defiance. Brown's face was swollen from the saber cuts to his head.

The grand jury swiftly brought in four indictments against Brown, including treason against Virginia, slave insurrection, and two counts of murder. When asked for a plea, John Brown stood and said, "If you seek my blood, you can have it at any moment without this mockery of a trial."[4]

William Lloyd Garrison

William Lloyd Garrison was a Massachusetts journalist who worked for many social reforms. He fought for women's rights, world peace, and abolition. In 1831, he founded *The Liberator*, a passionately antislavery newspaper. Fighting slavery became the focus of Garrison's life. Garrison hated slavery so much that he publicly burned a copy of the U.S. Constitution. Because it permitted slavery, he called the document a "covenant with death and an agreement with hell."[5]

Two Virginia lawyers, Lawson Botts and Thomas Green, were appointed to handle Brown's defense. The trial would begin the following day.

Several days after the attack on Harpers Ferry, with the initial shock wearing off, the Northern press was divided on the issue of John Brown. Abolitionist William Lloyd Garrison called the Harpers Ferry raid "Misguided, wild and apparently insane."[6] The widely respected *New York Tribune*, edited by Horace Greeley, an antislavery activist, suggested that the events in Kansas had driven poor John Brown mad.

Support for "A True Hero"

But there were other voices taking a much different view. Ralph Waldo Emerson called Brown "a true hero," and

Two militiamen assisted Brown, still suffering from his wounds, in standing in the courtroom when the indictments were brought against him.

hoped he might escape from the Charles Town jail.[7] Henry David Thoreau was among the most outspoken of Brown's supporters. He called John Brown a "'saintly hero,' the one person in America [with] Right on his side."[8] Thoreau described Brown in glowing terms—a strong, virtuous man "willing to [give] his life for the liberty of millions of enslaved [black people]." Thoreau denounced Brown's enemies as evil. Thoreau condemned the government of the United States that would "kill the liberators of the slave."[9] On October 20, 1859, Thoreau spoke on behalf of Brown in the Concord town hall to a sympathetic crowd.

On October 26, armed guards and cannons surrounded the Charles Town courthouse. There were rumors from the beginning that John Brown's friends would try to rescue him. The wounded Aaron Stevens lay on a mattress in front of the judge's bench. John Brown lay on a cot near him. Copeland and Green sat behind them. John Brown was tried first, so the others were taken back to jail.

John Brown asked for a delay in the trial because he still suffered from his injuries. A kidney wound especially bothered him. The wounds to his head had affected his hearing as well. The request was denied. John Brown then pled not guilty to all the charges against him.

When the trial resumed the next morning, John Brown seemed stronger. He walked without assistance, but he was still frail. He lay down on the cot except when he addressed the court.

An Informal Setting

Hundreds of spectators crowded into the courtroom. As was customary at that time, it was an informal atmosphere. The people ate peanuts, tossing the shells on the floor. There were so many discarded shells on the floor that when the lawyers walked around, they made crunching sounds. The men smoked cigars, and clouds of smoke filled the room. Other men chewed tobacco, spitting all over the floor.

In the disorderly courtroom, some of the spectators loudly cursed John Brown. The state prosecutor, Charles B. Harding, was a heavyset man with a wild beard. He rose to make his points, then he sat down, putting his

This sketch by Porte Crayon shows the courtroom during Brown's trial. Brown is in the center, lying on a cot. Hundreds of spectators crowded the courtroom.

feet up on the table in front of him. During some of the testimony, Harding fell asleep. Judge Andrew Parker, who presided over the trial, also tilted back in his chair, propping up his feet. The militiamen marched up and down the aisles, rifles at the ready.

During most of the trial, John Brown lay on his cot with his eyes closed. He seemed indifferent to the activities going on around him. When it was time for Brown to speak, he made his points clearly. He wanted the court to know that he attacked Harpers Ferry for a noble purpose—he wanted to free the slaves. He admitted he had taken hostages, but he insisted he had treated them well. Colonel Lewis Washington supported this claim. He had not been mistreated. Brown said he was sorry men had died as a result of the raid on Harpers Ferry, but he did not plan for that to happen.

The Insanity Plea

Brown's lawyers decided the only way they could save their client was to convince the court that he was insane. The lawyers produced evidence of insanity in Brown's family. It had afflicted his aunt, that woman's daughter, the son and daughter of Brown's uncle, and others. The lawyers also pointed to the fact that, as a child, John Brown grieved for an undue length of time over the death of a pet squirrel and this proved him to be of unsound mind.[10]

John Brown strongly rejected the plea of insanity and insisted he had not approved of his lawyers using that as a defense. He said he saw such an effort to save his life by claiming insanity as something he viewed with "contempt." The insanity plea was then dropped.[11]

Another lawyer, young Bostonian George Henry Hoyt, joined John Brown's defense team. But there was never any doubt about the outcome of the case. Everyone, including Brown, knew this. Yet Brown remained calm. When he was taken from the courtroom to the Charles Town jail, he slept soundly, and wrote long, detailed letters to his friends and family.

The closing arguments in the case were made on October 27, 1859. Hoyt argued that Brown was not from Virginia so he could not have committed treason against Virginia. Hoyt pointed out that John Brown could not be convicted for causing a slave insurrection since none had taken place. That may have been Brown's intent, but it did not happen. Finally, Hoyt said that Brown had not committed murder at Harpers Ferry. The men who died were casualties of war—John Brown's war against slavery. They were battle deaths, not murder, Hoyt insisted. It would be like accusing soldiers of murder for killing the enemy. The deaths were sad, but unavoidable, Hoyt argued. Hoyt was eloquent and he raised important points. But this court was not concerned with the finer points of the law.

The Verdict

During the closing arguments, John Brown lay on the cot with his eyes closed. The jury went out to deliberate. They were out for forty-five minutes. They came back and delivered the verdict: "Guilty of treason, and of conspiring and advising with slaves and others to rebel, and of murder in the first degree."[12]

John Brown turned to adjust his blanket, and stretched quietly. He said nothing. There was total silence in the courtroom. Brown was eventually taken back to the Charles Town jail. Sentencing was set for November 2.

On October 31, John Brown wrote a letter to his wife. He lamented the deaths of their sons, Oliver and Watson. He acknowledged he had been convicted on all counts and likely

> "I feel quite cheerful in the assurance that God reigns; and will overrule all for his glory & the best possible good."

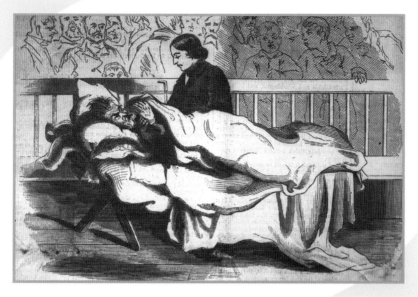

A young lawyer from Boston, George Henry Hoyt, gave the closing argument for John Brown during the trial. This sketch shows Hoyt sitting next to Brown on the cot.

faced execution. But then he wrote, "Under all these terrible calamities; I feel quite cheerful in the assurance that God reigns; and will overrule all for his glory & the best possible good."[13]

John Brown never wavered in his belief in the righteousness of his actions. Replying to a question from Virginia Senator James Mason, author of the Fugitive Slave Act, about the raid at Harpers Ferry, Brown said, "I think, my friend, you are guilty of a great wrong to God and against humanity—I say it without wishing to be offensive—and I believe it would be perfectly right to interfere with you so far as to free those you wickedly and willfully hold in bondage."[14]

Under Sentence of Death

Judge Parker asked John Brown if he wished to give any reasons why a sentence of death should not be pronounced against him. John Brown stood up and gave an eloquent speech. He insisted that he did not want lives to be lost, or property destroyed. He only wanted to free slaves. He argued that he did not work for the rich and powerful, or even for his family and friends. He worked instead for the "despised poor." Brown concluded, "[I] was not wrong, but right. Now, if it is deemed necessary that I should forfeit my life for the furtherance of the ends of justice, and mingle my blood further with the blood of my children and with the blood of millions in this slave country whose rights are disregarded by wicked, cruel, and unjust enactments—I submit, let it be done!"[1]

Brown's speech circulated around the country. Later, Ralph Waldo Emerson called it one of America's two greatest speeches (the other would be Abraham Lincoln's Gettysburg Address in 1863). Beyond the United States, Brown's words appeared in European newspapers. Many people in Europe were dismayed that the United States still held millions of human beings in slavery. They were sympathetic to John Brown for what he had tried to do.

Judgment Day

Judge Parker sentenced John Brown to die by hanging on December 2, 1859. Brown showed no emotion. His calm stunned onlookers. His supporters were inspired to defend him even more strongly. On the day after his sentencing, John Brown added a few lines to the unmailed letter he had written to his wife on October 31: "P.S. Yesterday Nov 2d, I was sentenced to be hanged on 2 Decem next. Do not grieve on my account. I am still quite cheerful. God bless you all Your Ever J Brown."[2]

On November 8, before a large audience at Boston's Music Hall, Ralph Waldo Emerson delivered a lecture called "Courage." He said all honorable people were abolitionists. He called John Brown "That new saint than whom none purer or more brave was ever led by love of men into conflict and death."[3] This address by Emerson as well as others praising Brown's courage intensified strong feelings in the North.

Meanwhile, on the same day, John Brown wrote another letter to his wife. He assured her that his upcoming execution "will do vastly more toward advancing the cause I have earnestly endeavored to promote, than all I have done in my life before."[4]

> While John Brown had become a noble hero in the North, he was a devil to be feared and hated in the South.

While John Brown had become a noble hero in the North, he was a devil to be feared and hated in the South. Brown remained calm, receiving many visitors. He spoke to all of them, even those who saw him as a curiosity. The only people he refused to see were any Christian clergymen who defended slavery. He saw them as total hypocrites and he wanted nothing to do with them.

John Brown had spent most of his adult life fighting slavery. He loved the enslaved African Americans with a passion that few could understand and hardly any other white person shared. Their fate consumed most of his waking hours. Now he felt he was going to die for them and he felt no fear.

Panic in the South

As John Brown's reputation grew in the North, panic grew in the South. Southerners could not believe that a man who led an armed raid on Harpers Ferry in an

New York, 2, March, 1858,

My Dear Wife

I received yours of the 17th Feby
yesterday; was very glad of it, & to know that you had got the
$10. safe. I am having a constant series of both great encour
agements; & discouragements: but am yet able to say in view
of all "hitherto the Lord hath helped me." I shall send Sal
mon something as soon as I can; & will try to get you the ar
ticles you mention. I find a much more earnest feeling among
the colored people than ever before: but that is by no means uni
versal. On the whole the language of Providence to me would
certainly seem to say try on. I flatter myself that I may be able to go
& see you again before a great while; but I may not be able.
I long to see you all. All were well with John & Jason
a few days since. I had a good visit with Mr Sanborn at
Gerrit Smiths a few days ago. It would be no very strange thing if
he should join me. May God abundantly bless you all. No one
writes me but you.   Your affectionate Husband
                              John Brown

John Brown wrote many letters to his wife while in jail before his
execution. He wrote this earlier letter to his wife in 1858, a little
more than a year before the Harpers Ferry raid.

effort to end slavery could become a revered figure in the North. Many Southerners felt threatened. If this was how the people of the North felt, how much longer could the South hold on to the institution of slavery? How long before what happened at Harpers Ferry would be happening all over the South if abolitionists like Brown led violent raids? Brown had warned that bloodshed was the only way to end slavery. Now many in the South took his words seriously. They saw civil war as inevitable.

The jail where John Brown was held was poorly guarded. There were two small cellblocks surrounded by a fourteen-feet-tall brick wall. John Brown and Aaron Stevens shared a cell. Governor Wise received many threatening letters from people who admired Brown. Some threatened to storm the jail and set Brown free. Wise claimed he had received 3,600 letters. Brown himself in a November 21 letter to his wife noted a "disquietude" around the jail. He saw fires burning day and night in the distance. He feared his supporters would be blamed.[5]

John Brown developed a warm and friendly relationship with his jailer, Captain John Avis. Brown assured Avis he would not escape or be rescued by friends. Brown did not want to be rescued, and he never considered escaping. Brown told friends by letter to give up any idea of rescuing him. He told them he was filled with joy at the prospect of giving his life for the slaves. He did not want this taken from him. Brown believed that God decided everything and it was God's will that

This is the jail where John Brown was held prisoner in present-day Charles Town, West Virginia.

he should hang. It would greatly advance the cause of abolition.

A Nation Divided

In the South, hatred of John Brown turned into hatred of the Republican Party as well. Senator William Seward, a Republican from New York, was a special target. Seward gave a speech suggesting civil war was unavoidable over the issue of slavery. A group of men in the South offered a reward of fifty thousand dollars for Seward's head. Some Democrats in the North also criticized Seward. They said his speech had caused "terrible scenes of violence, rapine and death that have been enacted at the confluence of the Potomac and the Shenandoah," according to an editorial in the *New York Herald*.[6] Seward defended himself, saying that while John Brown was a sympathetic figure, what he had done at Harpers Ferry made his execution "necessary and just."[7]

U.S. Senator Salmon Chase from Ohio, another antislavery politician, called Brown "the truly good old man who was about to die for others."[8] Abraham Lincoln, running for president at the time but not yet the Republican nominee, told an audience in Leavenworth, Kansas, that "the attempt to identify the Republican party with the John Brown business was an electioneering dodge." He admitted that Brown showed "great courage," and "rare unselfishness," but that did not justify the violence he caused.[9]

John Brown continued to write letters after his sentence was pronounced. In one he said, "I am waiting the hour of my public *murder* with great composure of mind and cheerfulness. Feeling the strongest assurance that in no other possible way could I be used to so much advance the cause of God & of humanity."[10]

The only thing disturbing John Brown's serenity in the least was concern for his family. They were not wealthy and he worried how they would manage without him. He knew that the burden of raising the younger children would now fall entirely to Mary Brown. John Brown asked her to give the girls a "very *plain but perfectly practical* education for both *sons and daughters*." He praised knowledge of the broom, washtub, needle, spindle, and loom. But he also asked that his daughters Annie, Sarah II, and Ellen II receive "enough of the learning of the schools to enable them to transact the common business of life comfortably and respectably."[11]

John Brown's friends George and Mary Stearns wanted something to remember him by. They sent a sculptor, Edwin Brackett, to the Charles Town jail. He sat outside the cell and sketched John Brown, turning those sketches into an impressive white sculpture displayed in the Stearns's home.

More Kind Words for John Brown

As John Brown waited in his cell for his scheduled execution, praise continued to pour in. He received sympathetic letters and he answered many of them. Abolitionist Henry Ward Beecher wrote that Brown would be forever glorious after he died on the gallows. Henry David Thoreau relentlessly promoted Brown's cause. Thoreau referred to the letters Brown had written from prison as "meteor-like, flashing through the darkness in which we live. I know of nothing so miraculous in our history."[12]

Adding to the high emotion of the times, there was an unusual astronomical event on November 15, 1859. There were a series of brilliant meteor showers, and one tremendously bright meteor, which made a bright streak across the night sky, and then exploded in the morning sky. People from as far north as Albany, New York, and as far south as Virginia witnessed the strange fireworks in the sky. When the large meteor burst, it set off a series of explosions that sounded like a thousand cannons firing at once. Many saw this event as a grim omen. Like the bright meteor, Brown too was going toward his destruction, but his cause would live on. And there would be explosions of war to follow.

Reporters from many foreign countries came to Charles Town as the time of Brown's execution neared. Telegraphs had spread the story of the brave old man who was not flinching in the face of death.

John Brown saw himself as a liberator of the enslaved, but he also admitted he was a sinner. He knew there were dark deeds in his past but he hoped for God's mercy. "I sleep peacefully as an infant," he said. "If I am wakeful, glorious thoughts come to me, entertaining my mind."[13]

One Final Visit

Mary Brown had been thinking about visiting her husband ever since he was condemned to die. Brown said that although he would love to see her, he discouraged her visit. He listed many reasons, including financial. He did not want her to use up on travel what little money she had for herself and the children. Also, he feared she would be stared at and might feel uncomfortable. Finally, he wrote "the little comfort it might afford us to meet again would be dearly bought by the pains of a final separation."[14] However, Mary Brown was determined to see her husband one last time.

On December 1, the day before his scheduled execution, Mary Brown arrived in Charles Town.

The day before his execution, Mary Brown arrived to visit her husband in jail. The couple discussed funeral arrangements and John Brown's will.

A twenty-five-man cavalry guard led her carriage to the jail. At 3:30 P.M. she was allowed to enter her husband's cell. Mary and John Brown immediately embraced for several minutes. Then they separated and Brown asked his wife about the children. He told her to tell them their father had no regrets for what he had done and he expected his actions to produce good results.

The couple spent four hours together. Brown discussed the disposal of his body with his wife. He thought it should be burned on a woodpile to save money and Mary Brown should carry the ashes home in a box to be buried in North Elba. Mary Brown refused to consider this. She wanted her husband's body placed in a casket to be taken north for a proper burial in North Elba.

John Brown then went over his will with his wife. He wanted her to have all his personal property except for some things he specifically gave to his children. His surveyor's compass and all surveying equipment he gave to John Brown Jr. His silver watch would go to Jason Brown. To Owen would go the double-spring opera glass (small binoculars) and fifty dollars. Salmon was also to receive fifty dollars. His daughter Ruth would be given the old family Bible, which contained all the family records. Each of the children would receive a Bible, provided they could be bought for the three dollars each that Brown had set aside. Then John Brown told Mary what he wanted written on his tombstone: "John Brown, born May 9, 1800, was executed at Charlestown, Va. Dec. 2, 1859."[15]

Captain Avis let John Brown out of his cell and Mary and John Brown had dinner in Avis's own apartment at the jail. Brown then asked if his wife might be allowed to spend this last night of his life with him. This request was refused. Mary Brown returned to the Wager House Hotel in Harpers Ferry. She did not want to be in Charles Town when the execution of her husband was carried out. She could not bear that.

10

Death and Aftermath

December 2, 1859, was a clear and mild day in Virginia. John Brown awoke in his cell and began reading from the Bible as he normally did. He made a few more bequests to his survivors and friends. In gratitude for his great kindness through-out the imprisonment, Brown gave Captain Avis his Sharps rifle.

At 7:00 A.M. the carpenters began carrying planks to a thirty-five-acre field on Rebecca

Hunter's farm in southeast Charles Town. There they built the scaffold. The platform was six feet high and twelve feet wide. There were twelve railed steps leading up near the front of the platform. The carpenters cut a hole and attached a trapdoor on hinges. This would spring open when the condemned John Brown fell. The gallows were made of two stout posts and a crossbeam with an iron hook from which hung a rope noose made of hemp.

Final Moments

At 8:00 A.M., soldiers gathered around the Charles Town jail. Colonel Robert E. Lee was among them. No strangers were allowed in Charles Town that day to prevent a last-minute attempt to save John Brown. Three thousand soldiers guarded all access roads. Two lines of soldiers stood around the scaffold.

John Brown jotted down a final note to his wife. Then he said farewell to the other prisoners in the jail. He shook hands with them and gave them each a silver coin to remember him by. When he got to Aaron Stevens, who had been at his side for a long time, Stevens said, "Goodbye Captain. I know you are going to a better land." Brown replied, "I know I am."[1]

Brown was dressed in a black frock coat, black vest, black trousers, and a slouch hat. He wore red carpet slippers. Witnesses who saw him depart the jail said he appeared very calm. A famous painting shows John Brown, as he leaves the jail for his hanging, bending down and kissing a black child held in her mother's

John Brown walks out of the jailhouse as guards lead him to the scaffold, December 2, 1859. This is the famous painting that shows Brown kissing a black child. This event never happened.

arms. This event never took place. The soldiers around Brown would not let anyone near him.

The sheriff tied John Brown's arms behind his back at the elbows. He was placed in an open wagon for the trip to the scaffold. Two white horses pulled the wagon. Brown sat on a black walnut coffin for the ride. It was the coffin his body would be placed in after the hanging.

As the wagon rumbled over the countryside, the sun shone brilliantly. John Brown looked around and said, "This is a beautiful country."[2]

At the scaffold, Brown was helped down from the wagon by guards. Captain Avis stood nearby. As Brown began to mount the steps to the gallows, he stopped and turned to Avis. "Sir," Brown said, "I have no words to thank you for your kindness."[3]

> **"I am ready at any time. Do not keep me waiting."**

One of the witnesses was Thomas J. "Stonewall" Jackson, who became a famous Confederate general during the Civil War. He said of Brown, "he ascended the scaffold with apparent cheerfulness," adding, "he behaved with unflinching firmness."[4]

John Brown's hat was removed and a white linen hood was put over his head. His legs were tied together. Asked if he wanted a signal to know when he would hang, he said, "I am ready at any time. Do not keep me waiting."[5]

With the noose around his neck, Brown stood on the trap door for about ten minutes. Then the rope overhead was cut and he fell about two feet. The noose around his neck had caused a one-inch gash. His spinal column snapped, and he was dead.

Funeral

With his death confirmed at 11:15 A.M., "black bunting was hung out, minute guns were fired, prayer meetings assembled, and memorial resolutions were adopted" in many Northern cities.[6] At Harpers Ferry, Mary Brown sobbed. A cavalry procession left the farm, taking the body to Harpers Ferry. There the coffin was opened to allow the widow to make sure it was her husband inside.

On December 3, Mary Brown traveled with her husband's body on the Baltimore & Ohio Railroad. At Philadelphia it was placed on a boat headed for New York. Funeral directors waited there to take Brown's body and restore it. He was dressed in fresh clothing and his appearance was improved. A public viewing was held in New York. An entire city block was filled with grieving people.

On December 7, the Browns finally reached North Elba. The children and other family members consoled Mary Brown. Annie, Sarah, and little Ellen, along with Salmon Brown, were there.

On December 8, a simple funeral was held. Brown's open coffin was placed on a table in front of the family home. Family and friends paid their respects. Lyman Epps, part African American and part American Indian, sang Brown's favorite hymn, "Blow Ye The Trumpet Blow." The Reverend Joshua Young of Burlington, Vermont, a family friend, gave a short sermon and prayed over the body. Then the casket was carried to the grave, which had been dug near a high rock, about fifty feet from the house.

After Brown's execution, Henry David Thoreau said, "He is more alive than ever he was. He is no longer working in secret. He works in public and in the clearest light that shines on this land."[7]

In the wake of his execution, a chorus of impassioned voices rang out across the nation. "Marvelous old man," cried abolitionist Wendell Phillips. "He has abolished slavery in Virginia."[8] On the other hand, Senator Andrew Johnson from Tennessee (later president of the

The Other Four

Four of John Brown's followers were hanged on December 16, 1859, for their part in the raid at Harpers Ferry. Two black men, Shields Green and John Copeland, went first at 10:30 A.M. Like John Brown had done, they walked firmly to the scaffold, and thanked their jailer for his kindness. Shields prayed aloud. The two white men, Edwin Coppoc and John Cook, walked to their execution with similar bravery. Like their leader John Brown, they faced death with the firm belief that their sacrifice had helped to end slavery.

United States after Abraham Lincoln's assassination in 1865) called Brown "a murderer, a robber, a thief, and a traitor."[9]

In Concord, Massachusetts, on the day of Brown's hanging, Henry David Thoreau praised his moral greatness. As mourning bells tolled, black Americans lauded Brown as their greatest champion.

Two weeks after John Brown's death, Mary Brown received some financial help from an organization of African-American women in New York. Other friends also extended help.

The Brink of Civil War

Throughout the South there was a frenzy of terror against anyone daring to praise what John Brown had done. All Northern newspapers were banned in some Southern cities. Men were stripped, tarred, and feathered, and some were lynched for expressing abolitionist ideas. A man in Mississippi who praised John Brown was thrown from a train. Many in the South were wild with rage that John Brown was being elevated almost to sainthood status in the North. They viewed Brown as a threat.

Many Southerners felt it was the beginning of the end of their way of life. The honor given John Brown along with the likely election of Abraham Lincoln as president in 1860 drove the South into despair. Though Lincoln never promised to end slavery and did not support the extreme measures of John Brown, he was seen as an enemy.

Legacy of John Brown

After the death of John Brown, there was an outpouring of literature and music about him. *The Battle Hymn of the Republic* began to include new lyrics about John Brown's body in the grave while his soul went marching on. Frank Sanborn, one of The Secret Six, published a book, *The Life and Letters of John Brown.*

Frederick Douglass said, "If John Brown did not end the war that ended slavery, he did at least begin the war that ended slavery. If we look over the dates, places, and men for which this honor is claimed," there is no doubt that "John Brown began the war that ended American slavery and made this a free republic."[10]

John Brown remained a controversial figure. He used violence in his crusade against slavery. His actions at Pottawatomie Creek were murderous. His attack on Harpers Ferry was desperate and doomed to failure. But Brown believed he was justified because for two hundred years terrible violence had been visited on millions of slaves in the United States. They were beaten, branded, burned, and often killed. They were denied freedom, forbidden to marry, separated from their families, and treated as property.

> "If John Brown did not end the war that ended slavery, he did at least begin the war that ended slavery."

Modern historians give a more balanced view of John Brown than was current during his lifetime. He is now portrayed as neither saint nor demon. He was a man who saw terrible evil and tried to end it,

After John Brown's death, there was an outpouring of music, literature, and art about him. This mural with Brown at center is in the Kansas statehouse.

but he used violence to accomplish his goals. Whether or not his actions were justified will probably never be settled.

A Widow's Life

In 1863, Mary Brown, with her son Salmon and three daughters, moved from North Elba to northern California. She lived in several parts of California over the years. She had longed to return east to visit her husband's grave. In 1882, she finally got her wish. She visited John Brown's grave and traveled to several cities where she was received with kindness. She remained

Mary Brown (center) with two of her daughters. Mary Brown moved to California with her three daughters and Salmon in 1863. She did not get to visit her husband's grave until 1882. She died two years later.

loyal to her husband's memory, and said that in all she had suffered, losing nine of her thirteen children and her husband, "In these trials, God upheld me."[11]

Mary Brown lived with her youngest child, Ellen Brown Fablinger, in Saratoga, California, but she was closest to another daughter, Sarah Brown, who never married. They were like sisters. Sarah was at her mother's side when she died on February 29, 1884, at the age of sixty-seven. Only four of her children were alive at that time—Salmon, Annie, Sarah, and Ellen. Four of her stepchildren were also alive—John Brown Jr., Owen, Jason, and Ruth—from John Brown's first marriage.

A School for John Brown

Early in his life, John Brown dreamed of opening a school for African-American children. He never reached that goal. But on October 2, 1867, friends and admirers of John Brown opened Storer Normal School at Harpers Ferry. Students of all races and religions were welcome. Frederick Douglass served as trustee of the school, which served many African-American students.

W. E. B. DuBois held a conference of the Niagara Movement, a forerunner of the National Association for the Advancement of Colored People (NAACP), at Storer School. DuBois, a militant activist for African-American rights, said John Brown was "the man who of all Americans has perhaps come nearest to touching the real souls of black folk," adding, "John Brown was right."[12]

CHRONOLOGY

1800—John Brown is born on May 9 in Torrington, Connecticut.

1820—Marries Dianthe Lusk.

1821—John Jr. is born on July 25.

1823—Jason is born on January 19.

1824—Owen is born on November 4.

1827—Frederick is born on January 9.

1829—Ruth is born on February 18.

1830—Frederick II is born on December 21.

1832—Dianthe Brown dies in childbirth on August 10.

1833—John Brown marries Mary Day on June 14.

1834—Sarah is born April 11.

1835—Watson is born on October 7.

1836—Salmon is born on October 2.

1837—Charles is born on November 3.

November 7—Abolitionist Elijah Lovejoy is murdered.

1843—Four Brown children, Charles, Sarah, Peter, and Austin, die from dysentery.

December 23—Daughter Anne is born.

1845—Amelia is born on June 22.

1846—Sarah II is born on September 11.

1848—Ellen is born on May 20.

1854—Ellen II, John Brown's last child, is born on September 25; Kansas-Nebraska Act is passed.

1855—Moves to Kansas with his sons during "free soil" versus slave state turmoil; the "Bleeding Kansas" crisis.

1856—Leads raiding party that kills five proslavery settlers at Pottawatomie Creek; "Secret Six," a group of wealthy New Englanders, formed to finance antislavery activity.

1858—Leads eleven fugitive slaves from Missouri to freedom in Canada.

1859—Attacks Harpers Ferry on October 16.

October 18—Two sons, Watson and Oliver, are killed; John Brown captured.

October 27—Trial begins.

November 2—Condemned to death.

December 2—John Brown executed by hanging.

CHAPTER NOTES

CHAPTER 1
Escape to Canada

1. Otto J. Scott, *The Secret Six—John Brown and the Abolitionist Movement* (New York: Times Books, 1979), p. 277.
2. L.L. Kiene, "The Battle of the Spurs and John Brown's Exit from Kansas," *Kansas Historical Collections*, 1903–1904, vol. VIII, pp. 443, 449.
3. Ibid.
4. David S. Reynolds, *John Brown, Abolitionist: The Man Who Killed Slavery, Sparked the Civil War, and Seeded Civil Rights* (New York: Alfred A. Knopf, 2005), p. 287.

CHAPTER 2
Frontier Childhood

1. David S. Reynolds, *John Brown, Abolitionist: The Man Who Killed Slavery, Sparked the Civil War, and Seeded Civil Rights* (New York: Alfred A. Knopf, 2005), p. 30.
2. Owen Brown, "Owen Brown's Biography," in F. B. Sanborn, ed., *The Life and Letters of John Brown* (New York: Negro Universities Press, 1885), p. 8.
3. John Brown, "The Childhood of John Brown," in Sanborn, p. 15.
4. Ibid., p. 13.
5. Owen Brown, p. 8.
6. Reynolds, p. 33.
7. John Brown, p. 14.
8. Ibid.
9. Ibid.
10. Reynolds, p. 33.

CHAPTER 3
Marriages and Business Ventures

1. John Brown, "The Childhood of John Brown," in F. B. Sanborn, ed., *The Life and Letters of John Brown* (New York: Negro Universities Press, 1885), p. 17.
2. F. B. Sanborn, ed., *The Life and Letters of John Brown* (New York: Negro Universities Press, 1885), p. 37.
3. Otto J. Scott, *The Secret Six: John Brown and the Abolitionist Movement* (New York: Times Books, 1979), p. 99.

CHAPTER 4
Bleeding Kansas

1. David S. Reynolds, *John Brown, Abolitionist: The Man Who Killed Slavery, Sparked the Civil War, and Seeded Civil Rights* (New York: Alfred A. Knopf, 2005), p. 78.
2. Ibid.
3. William S. McFeely, *Frederick Douglass* (New York: W. W. Norton and Company, 1995), p. 186.
4. F. B. Sanborn, ed., *The Life and Letters of John Brown* (New York: Negro Universities Press, 1885), p. 66.
5. Reynolds, p. 104.
6. Sanborn, p. 44.
7. Joseph Newman, ed., *200 Years: A Bicentennial Illustrated History of the United States* (New York: U.S. News and World Report, 1973), p. 277.
8. Samuel Eliot Morison, *The Oxford History of the American People* (New York: Oxford University Press, 1965), p. 591.
9. Sanborn, pp. 255–256.
10. James McPherson, *Battle Cry of Freedom* (New York: Oxford University Press, 1988), p. 149.
11. Reynolds, p. 17.

CHAPTER 5
The Killings at Pottawatomie Creek

1. F. B. Sanborn, ed., *The Life and Letters of John Brown* (New York: Negro Universities Press, 1885), pp. 266–267.
2. Salmon Brown Letter, in Sanborn, p. 262.
3. Sanborn, p. 250.

4. Ibid.
5. Ibid., p. 364.
6. Ibid., p. 507.

CHAPTER 6
The Road to Harpers Ferry

1. F. B. Sanborn, ed., *The Life and Letters of John Brown* (New York: Negro Universities Press, 1885), p. 501.
2. Ibid., p. 502.
3. David S. Reynolds, *John Brown, Abolitionist: The Man Who Killed Slavery, Sparked the Civil War, and Seeded Civil Rights* (New York: Alfred A. Knopf, 2005), p. 299.
4. Sanborn, p. 540.
5. Hannah Geffert, "They Heard His Call," in Peggy A. Russo and Paul Finkelman, eds., *Terrible Swift Sword: The Legacy of John Brown* (Athens, Ohio: Ohio University Press, 2005), p. 27.
6. Sanborn, p. 540.
7. Reynolds, p. 308.

CHAPTER 7
The Attack

1. F. B. Sanborn, ed., *The Life and Letters of John Brown* (New York: Negro Universities Press, 1885), p. 554.
2. David S. Reynolds, *John Brown, Abolitionist: The Man Who Killed Slavery, Sparked the Civil War, and Seeded Civil Rights* (New York: Alfred A. Knopf, 2005), p. 327.
3. Ibid.
4. Otto J. Scott, *The Secret Six—John Brown and the Abolitionist Movement* (New York: Times Books, 1979), p. 292.

CHAPTER 8
The Trial

1. F. B. Sanborn, ed., *The Life and Letters of John Brown* (New York: Negro Universities Press, 1885), pp. 571–572.
2. David S. Reynolds, *John Brown, Abolitionist: The Man Who Killed Slavery, Sparked the Civil War, and Seeded Civil Rights* (New York: Alfred A. Knopf, 2005), p. 330.

3. Ibid., p. 332.
4. Sanborn, p. 573.
5. "William Lloyd Garrison, Prospectus Inaugural Editorial for *The Liberator* 1831," in *Wendell Phillips Garrison, William Lloyd Garrison, 1805–1878: The Story of His Life Told By His Children,* vol. 1 (New York: The Century Company, 1885), pp. 224–226, n.d., <http://history.hanover.edu/courses/excerpts/111garrison.html> (January 6, 2009).
6. Reynolds, p. 340.
7. Otto J. Scott, *The Secret Six—John Brown and the Abolitionist Movement* (New York: Times Books, 1979), p. 297.
8. Reynolds, p. 344.
9. Ibid.
10. Kenneth R. Carroll, "A Psychological Examination of John Brown," in Peggy A. Russo and Paul Finkelman, eds., *Terrible Swift Sword: The Legacy of John Brown* (Athens, Ohio: Ohio University Press, 2005), p. 129.
11. Sanborn, p. 574.
12. Ibid., p. 575.
13. "Letter dated October 31, 1859," *John Brown's Letters to His Wife, Mary Day Brown, from the Charlestown Prison,* n.d., <http://www.law.umkc.edu/faculty/projects/FTRIALS/johnbrown/brownprisonletters.html> (January 6, 2009).
14. Reynolds, p. 330.

CHAPTER 9
Under Sentence of Death

1. F. B. Sanborn, ed., *The Life and Letters of John Brown* (New York: Negro Universities Press, 1885), p. 585.
2. "Letter dated October 31, 1859," *John Brown's Letters to His Wife, Mary Day Brown, from the Charlestown Prison,* n.d., <http://www.law.umkc.edu/faculty/projects/FTRIALS/johnbrown/brownprisonletters.html> (January 6, 2009).
3. David S. Reynolds, *John Brown, Abolitionist: The Man Who Killed Slavery, Sparked the Civil War, and Seeded Civil Rights* (New York: Alfred A. Knopf, 2005), p. 366.
4. "Letter dated November 8, 1859," *John Brown's Letters to His Wife, Mary Day Brown, from the Charlestown Prison,* n.d., <http://www.law.umkc.edu/faculty/projects/FTRIALS/johnbrown/brownprisonletters.html> (January 6, 2009).

5. Ibid.
6. Doris Kearns Goodwin, *Team of Rivals, The Political Genius of Abraham Lincoln* (New York: Simon & Schuster, 2005), p. 227.
7. Ibid., p. 228.
8. Ibid.
9. Ibid.
10. Ibid., p. 226.
11. "Letter dated November 16, 1859," *John Brown's Letters to His Wife, Mary Day Brown, from the Charlestown Prison,* n.d., <http://www.law.umkc.edu/faculty/projects/FTRIALS/johnbrown/brownprisonletters.html> (January 6, 2009).
12. Reynolds, p. 383.
13. Ibid., p. 388.
14. "Letter dated November 8, 1859."
15. Sanborn, p. 617.

CHAPTER 10
Death and Aftermath

1. F. B. Sanborn, ed., *The Life and Letters of John Brown* (New York: Negro Universities Press, 1885), p. 625.
2. Ibid.
3. David S. Reynolds, *John Brown, Abolitionist: The Man Who Killed Slavery, Sparked the Civil War, and Seeded Civil Rights* (New York: Alfred A. Knopf, 2005), p. 396.
4. Thomas J. Jackson, "The Execution of John Brown: Eyewitness Account," *Virginia Military Institute Historical Research Center,* 2008, <http://www.vmi.edu/archives> (January 6, 2009).
5. Sanborn, p. 626.
6. Doris Kearns Goodwin, *Team of Rivals: The Political Genius of Abraham Lincoln* (New York: Simon & Schuster, 2005), p. 226.
7. Peggy A. Russo and Paul Finkelman, eds., *Terrible Swift Sword: The Legacy of John Brown* (Athens, Ohio: Ohio University Press, 2005), p. 83.
8. Reynolds, p. 401.
9. Ibid., p. 402.

10. "Frederick Douglas at Harpers Ferry," *Harpers Ferry National Historical Park*, June 2, 2005, <http://www.nps.gov/archive/hafe/douglass.htm> (January 6, 2009).

11. Sanborn, p. 497.

12. Reynolds, p. 495.

GLOSSARY

abolitionist—A person determined to end or abolish slavery.

armory—A placed where weapons and military equipment are stored.

bowie knife—A sturdy, single-edged hunting knife with part of the back edge curved to a point and sharpened.

Calvinist—A Protestant sect that called the Bible the source of all truth, whose followers believed that obeying God's law was more important than obeying man's law.

cobbler—A person who makes or repairs shoes.

dysentery—A disease caused by infection, often from bad food or water, that can cause vomiting, diarrhea, and sometimes death.

Fugitive Slave Act—Law passed by Congress in 1850 that required police and federal officials to arrest runaway slaves anywhere in the country.

insurrection—An act or revolt against civil authorities or a government.

lynching—An illegal killing by hanging.

printing press—A machine that produces printed copies.

Quakers—A religious group, outspoken against slavery that believed every human life is special and that all human beings are equal.

Sharps rifle—A rifle designed by Christian Sharps in 1848, used around the time of the Civil War.

surveyor—A person who measures and notes property lines

tannery—A place where the hides of animals are treated to convert them into leather.

treason—The offense of attempting by overt acts to overthrow the government to which the offender owes allegiance.

FURTHER READING

Becker, Helaine. *John Brown.* Woodridge, Conn.: Blackbirch Press, 2001.

Brackett, Virginia. *John Brown, Abolitionist.* Philadelphia: Chelsea House Publishers, 2001.

Doak, Robin Santos. *Slave Rebellions.* New York: Facts on File, 2006.

Giovanni, Nikki. *Lincoln and Douglass: An American Friendship.* New York: Henry Holt and Co., 2008.

McNeese, Tim. *The Abolitionist Movement: Ending Slavery.* New York: Chelsea House, 2007.

Wagner, Heather Lehr. *The Outbreak of the Civil War: A Nation Tears Apart.* New York: Chelsea House, 2009.

Young, Jeff C. *Bleeding Kansas and the Violent Clash Over Slavery in the Heartland.* Berkeley Heights, N.J.: MyReportLinks.com Books, 2006.

INTERNET ADDRESSES

John Brown and the Valley of the Shadow
   <http://www2.iath.virginia.edu/jbrown/>

John Brown's Holy War
   <http://www.pbs.org/wgbh/amex/brown/>

The Kennedy Farmhouse—John Brown
an American Abolitionist
   <http://www.johnbrown.org/toc.htm>

INDEX